—

THE WALL STREET ERA IS OVER

—

THE INVESTOR'S GUIDE TO CRYPTOCURRENCY AND DEFI, THE DECENTRALIZED FINANCE REVOLUTION

Written by the industry experts at **DeFiYield.App**

CONTENTS

CHAPTER I. PREFACE   **X**

CHAPTER II. INTRODUCTION   **14**

Who is *The Wall Street Era is Over* for?   **14**
How *The Wall Street Era is Over* Will Help You   **15**
The Crypto Backstory   **15**
    Bitcoin is Digital Gold   16
       Cryptocurrencies are Programmable Money   19
    Smart contracts Enable Trustless Relationships   20
    DeFi is Finance 3.0   21
The DeFiYield Story   **23**
MAIN TAKEAWAYS FROM INTRO   **24**

CHAPTER III. WHAT IS DEFI?   **26**

Key Concepts to Understand   **29**
    Custody and Self-sovereign Money   29
    Crypto Wallets   31
How to Access DeFi   **32**
    Understanding Wallets   32
    Buying Crypto for the First Time   33
    Using Your Bank to Buy Crypto   33
    Banks' and Regulators' View of Crypto   34
    'Hot' Wallets vs 'Cold' Wallets   35
    Wallet Security   35
    Popular Wallets You Can Use   36
       MetaMask   36
       Trust Wallet   37

Trezor 37

Ledger 37

Game Theory 37

Incentives 38

Memes 39

FUD (Fear, Uncertainty and Doubt) 40

Cycles 41

The Most important DeFi Protocols **42**

Lending and Borrowing Protocols 43

MakerDAO 43

Compound Finance 44

Asset Management Protocols 46

Yearn Finance 46

Exchange Protocols 50

Bancor 51

Uniswap 52

SushiSwap 53

Curve Finance 54

Balancer 56

dYdX 56

Injective Protocol 57

0x 57

PancakeSwap 58

Brokerage and Account Services 59

DeFiYield 60

Cross-chain Asset Management Dashboard 60

Derivative Protocols 61

Synthetix 61

Other Important Protocols and Projects 63

The Graph 63

Oracles 64

Chainlink 65

Decentralized Insurance 65

Seigniorage coins 66

Empty Set Dollar 66

Dynamic Set Dollar 66

Why the Seigniorage Coin Hype is Over (For Now) 67

How DeFi Protocols Earn Revenue **67**

Credit Monetization 70

Automated Market Maker (AMMs) 71

Automated Asset Management 72

Aggregators, Routers & Relayers   73
Additional Concepts to Understand   **73**
Decentralized Governance and DAOs   73
   How DeFi Uses Decentralized Governance and DAOs   75
   Benefits of Decentralized Governance for DeFi Users 78
Stablecoins   79
   Different Types of Stablecoin   80
      Fiat-backed stablecoins   80
      Crypto-collateralized stablecoins 81
      Synthetic stablecoins   82
      Interest-bearing stablecoins 82
      Algorithmic stablecoins   82
Token Standards   83
   ERC-20   84
   ERC-721   84
   ERC-1155   84
Liquidity Pool (LP) Tokens   85
Vampire Attacks   86
Black Swan Events   86
Flashbots   87
   The MEV Problem   87
   How Flashbots Solve the Front-running Issue   89
MAIN TAKEAWAYS FROM THIS CHAPTER   **90**

CHAPTER IV. THE DEFI INVESTORS RULEBOOK   **91**

The Three Types of DeFi Investors   **91**
The Cautious Investor   91
The Risk-on Investor   92
The Degen Investor   92
Approaches for Investing in DeFi   **93**
DeFi Investment Indicators Explained   **96**
Cyber Security Record   97
Team Record   97
Terms of Liquidity Pools   97
Impermanent Loss   98
Annual Percentage Yield (APY)   98
Additional Areas of DeFi Investment Research   **99**
Product Value   99
Opportunity Cost   100
Smart contract security   100

Team credibility and public profile 101
MAIN TAKEAWAYS FROM THIS CHAPTER **102**

CHAPTER V. WHAT IS YIELD FARMING? **103**

How does Yield Farming fit into DeFi? **103**
Where did Yield Farming come from? **104**
Types of Yield Farming **108**
Yield from Lending 109
Yield from Providing Liquidity 110
Yield from Governance Token Distributions 111
Yield from Other Token Distributions 112
Advantages of Yield Farming **113**
Higher Returns than in Traditional Finance 113
Different Risk Levels for Different Risk Appetites 114
No Intermediaries 114
No Suits 115
Accessibility 115
Diversity of Platforms 116
Composability 116
Fast Growth 117
Disadvantages of Yield Farming **118**
UX Barrier 118
Volatility of Cryptocurrency Markets 118
Complexity of Smart Contracts 119
Reliance on Gas Prices 119
FUD, Rumors, and Outright Lies 120
Scam Projects Abound 120
Hacker Attacks 121
Fraudsters Might Go Unpunished 121
Yield Farming Risks and Mitigation Strategies **122**
Funds Liquidation Risk 122
Impermanent Loss Turning Permanent 123
Rising Gas Fees on Ethereum 125
Flash Loan Attacks 126
The dYdX Attacks 128
The Value DeFi Attack 129
Code Weaknesses in Smart Contracts 130
The Deus Finance Smart Contracts 130
The Bundles Finance Smart Contracts 132
The Alpha Homora Case 133

Scam Projects   135
    The 'One-click Rugpool' Scam   135
    The YFFS Scam   137
    The Compounder Finance Scam (and How We Will Find the Scammer)   138
      How did the Compunder.finance scam work?   139
      What has BEEN the response?   140
      How will the scammer(s) be caught?   141
MAIN TAKEAWAYS FROM THIS CHAPTER   **144**

CHAPTER VI. HOW TO SUCCEED AT YIELD FARMING? 145

General Principles for Safe and Profitable Yield Farming   **145**
    Get in Early   146
    Don't be Scared by Market Inefficiencies   146
    Diversify Your Investments   147
    Do Your Own Research   147
    Think Independently   148
    Farm with a Large Budget   148
    Avoid High-volatility Times   149
    Monitor Whale Activity   149
    Learning from Experienced Yield Farmers   150
      Overview of the DeFiYield Team Strategy   150
      More Stories from our Yield Farming Journey So Far   151
    Ask the Community for Help   153
      What the DeFiYield Community Says about Yield Farming   154
    Use Full Suite of DeFiYield Tools   156
    Auditing Smart Contracts   156
      DeFiYield's Safety Commitment to Smart Contract Audits   156
      Our Approach to Auditing   157
        Understanding ownership   158
        Auditing specific functions   159
        The Mint Function   159
        The Migrate function   161
        Proxy Patterns   162
        The TransferOwnership function   162
        Timelocks   163
How DeFiYield Keeps You Safe   **164**
    Auditing Smart Contracts So You Don't Have To   165
    Notifying the Community When We Find Issues   165
    Helping Responsible Projects Fix Code Weaknesses   166

Recording Scams in the Biggest Database of its Kind   166
Providing a Suite of Tools to Keep You Safe   166
Building a Community of Reliable Yield Farmers   167
MAIN TAKEAWAYS FROM THIS CHAPTER   **168**

CHAPTER VII. THE FUTURE OF DEFI   **169**

Governance-enabled Growth   **169**
Avoiding Whale Manipulation   **170**
Cross-chain Solutions   **171**
Binance Smart Chain   **172**
Interoperability   **176**
Layer 2 Scalability   **177**
    Increasing DeFi Projects' Flexibility and Functional Updates of DeFi projects   **179**
    Uniswap V3   179
Project Partnerships   **180**
    The Yearn Finance Ecosystem   181
DEXes Extend Their Trading Tools   **182**
Adoption of Seigniorage Coins   **184**
NFTs   **185**
    The 2021 NFT Hype   185
      Record NFT Digital Art Sales   186
      Celebrity Endorsements   186
      Brands Getting in on NFTs   187
    The Future of NFTs   187
Security Concerns   **188**
MAIN TAKEAWAYS FROM THIS CHAPTER   **190**

CHAPTER VIII. WHY YOU SHOULD USE DEFIYIELD NOW   **191**

The Problems DeFiYield Solves for DeFi Users   **191**

CHAPTER IX. CONCLUSION   **193**

Time for Next Steps   **193**
It's Your Turn   **194**

CHAPTER X. GLOSSARY OF TERMS   **197**

I. PREFACE

On December 1st 2020, I lost $1,200,000.

This amount was just some of the $12,000,000 total that was lost in one of the biggest scams to hit the Yield Farming industry.

Since then, I have worked tirelessly to track down the scammer(s). I've employed the help of a blockchain investigation agency, built a community of over 600 victims, and filed claims in major finance jurisdictions around the world, including New York and London.

So why, you might ask, am I writing a book that encourages you to take part in an industry where a scammer can run off with other people's money?

The answer is simple. My losses only tell one small part of the story.

That's because Yield Farming is one of the most exciting trends to appear in the world of Decentralized Finance, or DeFi, which itself is revolutionising the entire global financial system.

It is an amazing industry, one that is made up of a community-driven ecosystem that has rewarded early adopters like Synthetix Spartan and YFI liquidity providers with 100x returns. It is an opportunity that is open to everyone and one that, I am sure, you can benefit from, if you go about it in the right way.

After all, DeFi is the place where you can make 100x or you can lose your life savings.

While the loss I suffered looks significant to many, there is every likelihood the scammer will be caught because of clues he/they left behind and resources I have put towards finding him/them.

Furthermore, these losses pale into insignificance when compared to the wealth I have created through Yield Farming. The opportunity to create that wealth for yourself is far from over.

While Yield Farming has grown exponentially in recent months, it is still a small niche within the wider world of cryptocurrencies. For anyone that feels to have missed out on the rise of Bitcoin or other established digital assets, Yield Farming is without doubt the place to be.

When I started my journey in crypto in 2013, I was trading Bitcoin on the handful of exchanges where it was possible to do so. As the industry grew, I took the opportunity to dive into Initial Coin Offerings (ICOs) from 2015 onwards. When I did, I often FOMOed into them without doing the necessary due diligence. Unsurprisingly, this resulted in my first experiences of scams.

This is something I've had to get used to over the years but I wish I'd been able to access the knowledge and guidance of experienced investors back then so I could have avoided many obvious pitfalls.

This book is my chance to help others do exactly that.

Even though I began Yield Farming having amassed years of crypto experience, I found it confusing. There is a lack of clear and structured information about the industry. It is not regulated by any authority and is akin to the Wild West in terms of a secure investment. Furthermore, its exponential growth turned anonymous developers into crypto hedge fund managers almost overnight. While they were happy to take and hold investors' funds, some feel no responsibility to do what's right.

Scams are frequent. Events that may mean nothing to you right now - such as arbitrage attacks, rug pulls, infinite minting, minting exploits, pulled liquidity and owner tampering - happen regularly and can result in Yield farmers losing millions.

I want Yield Farming to be safe for everyone.

This is why I have translated complex concepts of Yield Farming into simple and clear explanations that anyone can follow. This book empowers you to skip months of painful experience with scams and fake projects, by helping you to learn what to pay attention to when assessing different ones. The stories inside provide my personal insights about various real-world cases, collating all the information you need in one place.

Mark Cuban, a billionaire entrepreneur who is famous for building and investing in internet companies before many believed the technology would transform the world, says this of DeFi:

"DeFi is really straightforward if you try it and you understand the principles behind it."*

I totally agree with this statement. To understand DeFi and to benefit from Yield Farming, you need to try it for yourself. This book will help you to understand the principles behind it, while the tools and resources we make available through DeFiYield.App will help you step into this industry with confidence.

This book aims to lower the barriers of entry to the industry, so more people can engage in DeFiYield Farming. It can help everyone from absolute beginners to adept farmers. If you want to understand the industry, to succeed at Yield Farming and to remain safe while you do, this is the book for you.

* Mark Cuban said this on the Bankless video and podcast show, when he was interviewed for the episode 'Why DeFi is the Future', which was released in February 2021.

II. INTRODUCTION

Who is *The Wall Street Era is Over* for?

I wrote this book for anyone who wants to take advantage of the enormous opportunity that DeFi provides but is wary of the financial risks that come with it. As we delve deeper into the book's second half, we will thoroughly explore DeFi's Yield Farming sector (also known as liquidity mining).

You might be a complete novice who has never bought any cryptocurrencies before. Or you may be a fledgling Yield farmer who wants to learn from an established player who has seen it all. Perhaps you're somewhere in between.

Wherever you're starting from, this book has been written to give you all the background knowledge and basic principles you need to understand DeFi. From there, we will provide you with the necessary tools to start Yield Farming as soon as possible.

Some basic understanding of financial fundamentals and an existing interest in cryptocurrencies is required. It's OK if your knowledge in these areas is not very advanced, however. The very fact that you want to understand DeFi more fully is a sure sign that this book is for you.

How *The Wall Street Era is Over* Will Help You

The aim of this book is to bring clarity and confidence to anyone who wants to enter the DeFi industry. By reading it, you will significantly reduce the risk to which you are exposed in this innovative new industry, particularly if you want to progress to Yield Farming.

As I explained, I have been scammed in this industry – and I've also earned even greater profits from it. I want to share my stories, experiences, and the lessons I've learned along the way, so you can be successful in DeFi yourself.

I'll walk you through the history of DeFi, the forces at play within the market, the participants who are involved, and the metrics you need to track. Then I'll introduce you to the primary DeFi projects that you should start with for Yield Farming.

Most importantly, I'll explain how my colleagues and I at DeFi Yield have used our smart contract auditing experience to select the safest projects and to warn Yield farmers away from scams. In the process, I'll also reveal some exclusive information about the investigation into the scam I mentioned. This information has never been made public before – it will reveal how the scammer will be caught.

Finally, we'll look beyond the here and now. We will identify the most important trends to keep an eye out for, so you'll be empowered to continue your DeFi journey long into the future.

The Crypto Backstory

If the whole world of crypto is relatively new to you, it's important to understand some of DeFi's main narratives before you dive in.

Let's begin with a short description of where DeFi fits into the wider crypto environment industry. Then we'll work through the details of what this means

> *"DeFi occurs on smart contract platforms.*
> *Smart contracts use programmable money to*
> *exchange value between entities in a trustless*
> *manner. This process can trace its evolution*
> *back to the original cryptocurrency, Bitcoin."*

This statement may not make complete sense to you if you are new to crypto, but it contains important basic concepts. Some of these concepts are firmly established, while others continue to be the subject of intense debate. All of them should be more clear by the end of this introduction and provide you with a foundation that allows you to really dig into DeFi.

Of course, if you want to learn more about these key topics, we encourage you to continue with your own research. The world of cryptocurrency and DeFi moves very fast! While we believe DeFi fundamentals will remain consisten t, you can expect new innovations to build on each other and constantly reshape the game.

Bitcoin is Digital Gold

Even though Bitcoin was introduced to the world "as a peer-to-peer electronic cash system," most people now think of it as more akin to "digital gold." Why is that?

Probably the most important reason for that mindset is the fact that Bitcoin has a digitally provable limited supply, which makes it a good store of value over the long-term – the same way that many people view investing in precious metals such as gold and silver.

The Bitcoin codebase is open source, and anyone can check and verify it. While they take some experience to understand, "block explorers" are online tools that provide this very public view of blockchains (such as this one at https://www.blockchain.com/explorer).

Bitcoin's code states that only 21 million bitcoins will ever be in the total circulating supply (Bitcoin trades as BTC on crypto exchanges). Another element of the supply is the number of bitcoins that will be mined, which essentially means the rate at which new bitcoins are added to the currency's total circulating supply. The mining rate is also established in the code and is reduced every four years.

It's important to contrast the fixed supply of Bitcoin with the considerably more fluid supply of a regular fiat currency. Let's look at the US dollar as an example: The total number of dollars in circulation has increased massively in recent years and will likely do so into the future as well. This increase is possible simply because the US Federal Reserve can choose to print more money at will, without any technical constraints or limits on its ability to do so.

The starkly different supply dynamics between Bitcoin and the US dollar is one reason people think of Bitcoin as more like gold than like a central bank fiat currency. Bitcoin's finite supply, and the fixed rate at which new assets are produced, gives Bitcoin and gold some key similarities. Like Bitcoin, gold is limited in supply and can only be mined (from the Earth) at a fairly consistent rate.

These characteristics have resulted in gold being classified as a Store of Value for centuries, if not millennia. The term "store of value" refers to assets, commodities, or currencies that can be saved, retrieved, and exchanged with the expectation that they will maintain their value into the future. (Contrast this with avocados, for example, which are tasty and desirable but have a short shelf life before they spoil.)

Many people now view Bitcoin as a Store of Value and therefore refer to it as digital gold. When you consider that Bitcoin's market cap is just 5-10% of gold's market cap at the time of this writing, you can see why these same people also believe that cryptocurrency's price has plenty of room to grow.

Financial Asset Market Cap

As of 11 April 2021

#	Name	Market Capitalization ($ millions)
1	Financial Assets	$266,917,000
2	Cash	$39,000,000
3	Gold	$11,938,404
4	Bitcoin	$1,124,145

DeFiYield.App

Gold and Bitcoin both represent a Store of Value, but Bitcoin has several advantages over gold. These include:

- Bitcoin can be transferred over the Internet, whereas gold requires trucks, planes, and armored personnel to move it securely.

- Gold is very expensive to move and store, while transferring and storing Bitcoin is much cheaper.

- Verifying gold's authenticity prior to purchase requires handling, weighing, and testing it (or paying someone else to do this for you). Bitcoin's authenticity can be verified simply by checking the globally available ledger – the blockchain – to confirm your seller's crypto ownership claims.

Cryptocurrencies are Programmable Money

The Bitcoin narrative is extremely powerful in the crypto community. It has an amazing origin story, springing into the world from a 2008 white paper written by the pseudonymous software developer Satoshi Nakamoto. Officially launched in 2009, Bitcoin was the first-ever cryptocurrency, in that it relied on cryptography to control the money's creation and transfer it in a secure way.

Bitcoin is an incredible achievement in so many ways. As open source software, it was envisioned by Satoshi as "a peer-to-peer electronic cash system." Bitcoin represents the first practical application of blockchain, which was brilliantly combined with cryptography to unlock completely unprecedented powers.

Despite its many breakthroughs, it's also fair to say that Bitcoin has limitations. The Bitcoin community has chosen to keep this monetary network as secure as possible. However, it is clear now that this security has come at the expense of other key considerations, including scalability and extendability.

Bitcoin is a programmable money. It is code, with a set of rules embedded within it, such as the 21 million cap on how many bitcoins can be minted. All of this code comes together into a monetary system existing purely on a computer network. Working together 24/7, this global computer network reaches consensus (or agreement) on a shared ledger of transactions, which is the Bitcoin blockchain in action.

However, even in the early days, many developers saw the potential for expanding the foundational technologies at the heart of Bitcoin. They saw how blockchain, digital assets, and consensus could be harnessed to do much more than simply transfer value in the form of bitcoins.

Thus began the second-most-valuable cryptocurrency by market cap, Ethereum (trading as ETH), in 2015. Its co-founder, Vitalik

Buterin, and other early Bitcoin advocates admired what Bitcoin had achieved and wanted to develop something different. With Ethereum, the vision was a cryptocurrency that could be more than merely a payment system or a Store of Value. With Ethereum, Buterin and his colleagues saw the opportunity to create a crypto that could execute "smart contracts," and therefore empower the creation of decentralized applications.

Now, Ethereum has over a million developers working on it, and the vast majority of the DeFi ecosystem is built on it. NFTs, or non-fungible tokens (which certify the uniqueness of digital art, music, and much more) are also built on the Ethereum blockchain.

This evolutionary process, which involves blockchain developers taking what has come before and using it to start a new project, is constantly unfolding. It works because most decentralized technologies are open source and available for anyone to see and build on. As a result, we now have many different blockchain networks with their own cryptocurrencies and objectives.

Cryptocurrency projects vary wildly in quality, but one common principle they share is a basis in programmable money, which means they do not use the physical money we have been accustomed to for centuries (fiat currency such as coins and bills, or their digital equivalents). Instead, they can be programmed to have specific characteristics such as supply limits, transaction recording, and transfer protocols that their developers choose and write into the codebase.

Smart contracts Enable Trustless Relationships

One of the main differences between Bitcoin and Ethereum, apart from monetary characteristics such as the supply of coins, is that Ethereum is far more extendable than Bitcoin.

- With its extendable qualities, Ethereum moves well beyond

simply being a Store of Value asset like Bitcoin. It also represents a platform for a whole new digital economy. Ethereum allows developers to build smart contracts that interact with the network and automate interactions between different parties in a trustless way.

A smart contract is simply code that lays out what will happen if certain criteria are met. The relationships they enable almost always involve the transfer of value, in the form of digital assets. These relationships and transfers play out based purely on what is programmed in the code, which is what is meant by a trustless relationship.

Trustless relationships occur when two entities – which could be two individuals but might just as well be two smart contracts – exchange value via a smart contract.

They do not exchange this value on the basis of the established social norm – trusting the person or organization on the other side of the transaction. Instead, the value exchange is governed solely by the smart contract code.

This kind of contract may sound a little theoretical, but it's a fundamental function of DeFi. At their best, smart contracts remove personal judgment from the process, which eliminates human error and is why smart contracts can run in an extremely efficient, frictionless manner. These contracts are already vastly reducing the cost and complexity of many industries – from decentralized finance, to insurance, to digital art.

Many DeFi concepts have proven to be vastly profitable. DeFi provides the best example of how smart contracts successfully interact. They form a dynamic marketplace that is growing every day.

DeFi is Finance 3.0

At DeFiYield, we see DeFi as Finance 3.0. It combines the elements of:

- Programmable money,
- Smart contracts
- Trustless relationships.

Together, these elements have formed a new, open financial system that will replace traditional finance. Here's how we got to this point.

Finance 1.0 can be thought of as the world of gold and central banks, which most people see as the foundation of today's traditional financial system. For roughly 400 years from the mid-17th Century, we used money, in the form of coins and bills, that was backed by gold and issued by nation states. In the 20th century, the link between the coins and bills we use and the gold that backed them disappeared. In the United States, for example the U.S. dollar ceased to be connected to gold in 1971; it was the end of the "gold standard."

Next was **Finance 2.0,** which has evolved with the internet and has enabled money's digitization. Now, fintech applications like Stripe, Revolut, Robinhood, and eToro leverage the internet. They have added an additional communications layer to Finance 1.0.

Monetary digitalization was a huge step forward, but Finance 2.0's potential for expansion has its limits. It's a sector primarily focused on allowing users to manage their money more easily with mobile apps. However, Finance 2.0 remains fundamentally centralized around nation states, commercial banks, and established institutions. Its outdated payment rails move assets and wealth with inefficient systems.

Finance 3.0 is totally different. It uses programmable money, not state-issued fiat currencies. It uses open, decentralized networks, not closed payment rails. It does not need commercial banks to operate as gatekeepers, because anyone can be their own bank.

Crucially, Finance 3.0 is permissionless and peer-to-peer, which means that anyone, anywhere can take part, regardless of their race, religion, gender, ethnicity, or country of birth. It is a truly egalitarian system that opens finance up to the whole world, not only a few big economies.

IIn Finance 3.0:

- No middlemen act as central points of control.
- You do not need to deposit your assets in a bank.
- You can be your own bank in a non-custodial system.

In other words, you own all your data. You do not need to hand it over to large, centralized institutions in order to gain access to the system. Finally, it is permissionless and uninterrupted, so you can transact at any time, with whomever you want. Regulatory changes in DeFi are always a possibility, however; therefore, we will update the book as often as possible.

This is Finance 3.0. It's a revolution. It's DeFi.

The DeFiYield Story

DeFiYield is your entry point into DeFi. We offer everything you need to access the wide world of DeFi. It's a place to participate in Yield Farming as safely as possible.

We also offer many community tools to support DeFi experts and newcomers alike. We provide how-to DeFi guides, and the largest Telegram group for advanced Yield Farmers. We'd love to hear from you! Stay up to date with the latest Finance 3.0 tools, news, and insights by visiting us at https://DeFiYield.app/

MAIN TAKEAWAYS FROM INTRO

IAt the end of each chapter, you will find a highlights section that provides a recap of what has been covered.

Bitcoin

Bitcoin is a programmable money with limited supply that performs all the classic functions of money: store of value, means of exchange, unit of account. Bitcoin is now considered 'digital gold" and its circulating supply cannot be controlled by any centralized body.

Programmable money

Cryptocurrency projects vary wildly in quality, but one common principle they share is a basis in programmable money. All cryptocurrencies are code with a set of rules embedded within them. Ethereum was created after Bitcoin as a crypto that could execute 'smart contracts' and therefore empower the creation of decentralized applications.

Smart contracts

Smart contracts are lines of code that allow you to automatically execute terms of certain agreements and processes on a blockchain. They automate interactions between different entities and make them 'trustless,' meaning third parties are not necessary to make sure interaction conditions are met.

DeFi is Finance 3.0

Finance 1.0 was a financial system that fully relied on central bank regulation, commercial bank operations and a fiat currency that was backed by actual gold reserves. Finance 2.0 featured the digitalization of commerce, payments and banking services, with intermediaries present across all layers of the financial system. Finance 3.0 is based on programmable money, smart contracts and trustless peer-to-peer operations that make up an entirely new, open and decentralized financial system.

III. WHAT IS DEFI?

To understand what DeFi is, let's start with another short description of this term. Then we'll use a practical example of how traditional finance markets work, so we can compare the similarities and contrast the differences.

Decentralized finance (a.k.a., DeFi), is an ecosystem of protocols, applications, investors, and traders that use smart contracts to perform financial transactions in an open, permissionless, and transparent way.

A good way to understand this concept is through your previous experience of traditional financial markets. If you think of any marketplace, whether it is a financial exchange like the New York Stock Exchange or a consumer app like eBay, you have three main entities working together: the buyer, the seller, and the marketplace itself.

- The buyer accesses the exchange in order to find a seller.
- The seller accesses the exchange to find a buyer.
- The exchange works in the middle to facilitate these requirements.

As a buyer or seller, you might have reasons to want the exchange to know and hold information about you and the entity on the other side of your trade. However, the fundamental innovation at the heart of smart contracts is that you don't need them to know and hold this information, as long as you are able to make the trade on the terms you want.

With a smart contract, you (or anyone or anything) can make a trade without knowing who you are trading with, and without the smart contract holding or using any information about you. It is a trustless relationship, because all that it relies on is the smart contract's code performing as designed.

This trustless relationship is the key dynamic at the heart of the decentralized finance (DeFi) industry right now.

How does DeFi differ from traditional finance?

In DeFi, smart contracts facilitate relationships in the same way that banks, payment providers, financial exchanges, and other intermediaries have done for centuries in traditional finance. For example, a DeFi protocol, Compound Finance, does this for lending and borrowing, as well as receiving digital assets from one entity and lending them to another, while an interest payment incentivizes the process.

Countless examples of smart contracts replicate other areas of traditional finance, with more arriving every day. You only have to think of the size, power, and influence of traditional finance markets to see why such excitement surrounds DeFi's potential.

Let's compare some key components of traditional finance (Finance 1.0) versus DeFi (Finance 3.0) to see how they differ:

Traditional Finance vs. Decentralized Finance

	Traditional 1.0		Decentralized 3.0
Type of money	**Fiat**	→	**Cryptocurrency**
	For example: dollars, euros, yuan and yen.		For example: Bitcoin (BTC), Ethereum (ETH), stablecoins and tokens.
Money issuance	**Controlled by the state**	→	**Auditable in the code**
	Central banks decide how much new money to print, based on senior bankers' decisions.		The amount of tokens/coins that are minted is specified in each crypto's code for anyone to assess and understand.
Money transfer	**Closed payment rails**	→	**Open payment networks**
	Payment networks, such as SWIFT, are controlled by commercial banks and used to transfer funds between agreed-upon entities.		Crypto is transferred quickly and cheaply to anyone you choose, without prejudice and without any requirement for middlemen.
Lending and borrowing	**Controlled by banks**	→	**Enabled by smart contracts**
	Restricted to the customers of major commercial banks, like HSBC, who the bank deems "credit-worthy."		Any individual can lend or borrow in DeFi using their crypto, without the need for a bank to approve them.
Exchanges	**Require middlemen**	→	**Automated and P2P (Peer-to-Peer)**
	To trade stocks, you need to access brokerages, like Charles Schwab, and exchanges, like the Nasdaq.		Decentralized exchanges enable buyers to interact directly with sellers (peer-to-peer) and remain in control of their funds.

 DeFiYield.App

Not only early adopters and tech aficionados are getting excited about DeFi.

Many of the world's biggest banks dismissed Bitcoin as a sham in 2017 and actively discouraged their clients from investing in cryptocurrencies. Now, they are rushing to hold (or "custody") digital assets on their clients' behalf so they can be saved, traded, and transacted. For example, Jamie Dimon, CEO of JP Morgan, called bitcoin a "fraud" in 2017, yet the bank is launching a debt instrument of Bitcoin proxy stocks in 2021.

By every measure, DeFi usage is increasing. As the table below shows, both the Total Value Locked (or TVL, which shows the total dollar amount of all coins and tokens that have been deposited in DeFi protocols) and the number of DeFi users has grown rapidly, starting in mid-2020.

Total value locked & users in DeFi

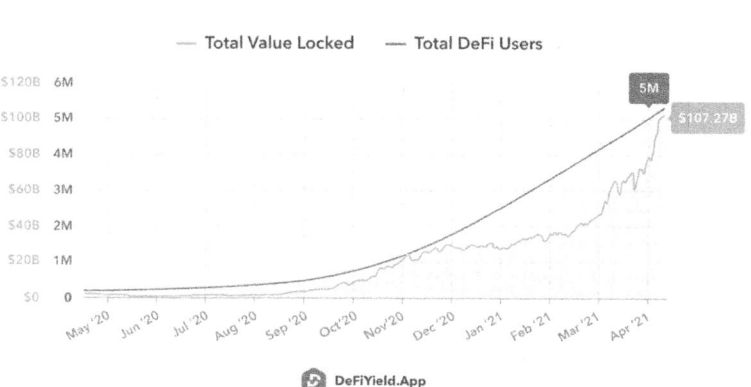

Even though DeFi usage is increasing, the total number of users around the world in March 2021 was just 1.5 million. Therefore, if you are reading this book to become a DeFi user, you will definitely be part of the first 1% of early adopters in this innovative and disruptive new industry.

Key Concepts to Understand

Custody and Self-sovereign Money

You might think that you do, but in reality, you rely on your bank to give you access to that money, as per the agreement you signed when you deposited your funds. That setup may seem to be the same as owning it; however, your confidence is probably because you are lucky enough to live in a country where you haven't experienced the shock of being able to access your money on one day but not the next.

The reality is that a commercial bank can and does stop individuals from accessing their money for all kinds of reasons. One of the most concerning scenarios for a customer is when a country's central bank directs its banks to block people's access to their funds.

If banks don't stop you outright from accessing your money, they might instead put restrictions on what you can do with it. You only need to search for terms like "bank run" or "capital controls" to see several examples from the last 50 years of countries that have put arbitrary controls on what their citizens can do with their own money.

This disturbing scene played out in Cyprus in 2013, for example, when lenders warned that emergency liquid assistance (ELA) authorized by the European Central Bank was about to be cut, causing a potential run on the banks. Cypriot banks went into a two-week shutdown to head off a bank run that would drain them of their capital, while pension funds and other large depositors lost uninsured savings.

Cryptocurrencies are very different. They are the financial manifestation of the concept of self-sovereignty, also known as self-ownership, which refers to the right and ability to have exclusive control over your own life. Cryptocurrency represents self-sovereign money because only you control your crypto through an increasingly easy-to-use process of cryptographic signatures.

Because of its decentralized nature and the fact that it is not government-issued, cryptocurrency needs no intermediaries such as banks in order to buy, sell, and transact with it. This is the essence of the peer-to-peer electronic cash system that Satoshi Nakamoto pioneered when he created the first-ever cryptocurrency, Bitcoin. This self-sovereignty is also why crypto is a lifesaving resource for dissidents in totalitarian regimes, as well as for any citizens who do not trust how their country's finances are run, since it allows these people to transact with a currency that is borderless and valued globally.

Of course, you could choose to use centralized crypto exchange and custody services, such as Coinbase, to buy and store your cryptocurrencies. However, the drawback is that doing so not only leaves your funds under the control of a centralized institution that is regulated in much the same way that a bank is; it also doesn't allow you to enjoy the benefits of DeFi projects, which are built on highly decentralized platforms and protocols and have limited compatibility with centralized crypto exchanges.

Crypto Wallets

Crypto wallets are virtually as old as crypto itself. Satoshi Nakamoto released the very first wallet protocol – Bitcoin-Qt – in 2009, which was later rebranded as Bitcoin Core. Nostalgists will be pleased that it is still available for download at the Bitcoin.org website.

Broadly speaking, wallets are either "Hot" or "Cold":

- Hot wallets connect to the Internet (Web3.0 wallets like MetaMask).
- Cold wallets use secure physical devices to store crypto and private keys locally, with no internet connection (hardware wallets)

Hardware wallets are considered the safest way to store cryptocurrencies, but they still have vulnerabilities to keep in mind.

How to Access DeFi

In order to access DeFi, you will need three things:

1. The internet
2. A PC or smartphone
3. A DeFi wallet (also referred to as a crypto wallet or Web3 wallet)

OOnce you have all three, the final thing you'll need is some amount of a blockchain network's native token in your wallet, in order to pay for the transaction fees involved in DeFi.

These fees are also referred to as 'gas fees,' as they require some energy to be expended in order for the transaction to be recorded on the underlying blockchain. On the Ethereum network, the gas fees are charged in 'gwei,' which is the fractional unit of 'Ether,' the Ethereum network's native token.

Understanding Wallets

The wallet you use to access DeFi might be described as a crypto, DeFi, or Web3 wallet in different situations, but this is only because these are emerging, closely intertwined industries that are not clearly separated.

However you describe your wallet, the important thing to realise is that it is the main tool you use to interact with the decentralized applications (or dapps) built on blockchain networks that characterize the new Web3 paradigm.

The wallet you use is also referred to as a self-custody wallet because you are the only one who controls access to it. This setup is unlike a bank account, where you have access but only because the bank gives you access. In this way, wallets give you full control and responsibility.

More specifically, using a wallet ensures that:

- Your identity is not required

- Your personal data is never requested.

- Your transactions are not restricted.

- Only you can access your wallet.*

*The important additional point to note here is that if you start using your wallet to interact with DeFi, you will be giving the smart contracts that are within these dapps access to your wallet.

Buying Crypto for the First Time

Although DeFi provides an autonomous, decentralized financial ecosystem, the reality is that most people still need to make their first step into it by converting the fiat currency they hold (such as dollars, euros, or pounds) into a cryptocurrency or token (like bitcoin or ether).

Some readers will understand this process and will have taken the necessary steps already. For those who have not, it will more than likely involve sending some of the fiat currency you hold in your bank account to an account you have with a centralized cryptocurrency exchange, such as Coinbase or Binance.

In this situation, crypto exchanges are referred to as on/off ramps because they are the mechanism by which you go onto the crypto ecosystem or off of it back into the fiat system.

Using Your Bank to Buy Crypto

Before you try to transfer funds from your bank account to an exchange account to make your first purchase, you should be aware that many banks across the world do not allow transfers to cryptocurrency exchanges.

Furthermore, in 2021, reports circulated that banks which had not previously restricted transfers were changing their policies without warning. In some cases, these banks were also restricting other transactions and even closing accounts altogether. Therefore, to avoid any issues, always check to see whether your bank has any such restrictions.

Many of the digital or neo banks advertise themselves as 'crypto-friendly.' What this term actually means depends on the individual bank, but by doing some research, you may find one in your country that allows you to make transfers of this kind.

Banks' and Regulators' View of Crypto

Keep in mind that the regulatory situation is fluid, with many countries urgently reviewing their regulatory frameworks in order to keep pace with the crypto industry's staggering growth.

In the US, some positive regulatory signs have surfaced of late regarding banks' use of blockchain networks. In January 2021, the US Office of the Comptroller of Currency said the following:

"A bank may use stablecoins to facilitate payment transactions... including by issuing a stablecoin, and by exchanging that stablecoin for fiat currency. In this context, stablecoins function as a mechanism of payment, in the same way that debit cards, checks, and electronically stored value (ESV) systems convey payment instructions. Banks have long used cashiers' checks, travelers' checks, and other bearer instruments as a means of facilitating cashless payments."

This statement matters because of the leading position of the US economy, the US dollar, and the US banks within the global financial system. It could have a knock-on effect on regulators in other jurisdictions.

'Hot' Wallets vs 'Cold' Wallets

As interest in crypto markets and different blockchain networks has increased in recent years, a number of different wallet solutions have been developed to meet users' needs.

Broadly speaking, wallets are classed as 'hot' or 'cold.' A hot wallet is one that connects to the internet and makes it easy to interact with DeFi and other Web3 applications. A cold wallet is a physical device (often referred to as a hardware wallet) that stores private keys locally on the device. Cold wallets are generally considered the safest option because hardware wallets are rarely connected to the internet, thus reducing the potential for attacks. They use random number generation to create public/private keys and let you set your own PIN code and recovery phrase.

No verifiable hacks to hardware wallets have yet been confirmed, but you should still keep some vulnerabilities in mind. For example, vulnerabilities can occur if devices have been tampered with or compromised, so make sure to only use trusted brands and to buy directly from the manufacturer.

Also, you should consider the risk of a hardware wallet being damaged or lost.

Wallet Security

Wallet security is achieved through a private key and/or seed phrase. You alone are responsible for their safekeeping, so if you lose them, you lose your crypto.

To ensure this doesn't happen, you should follow some security best practice:

- Keep your private keys in a non-digital/manual record
- Keep a non-digital/manual record of your seed phrases

- Use multiple wallets to distribute your tokens and diversify your risk.

- When connecting to a DeFi dapp for the first time, use a test wallet that holds only small amounts of tokens (just enough for gas).

- Be aware of and avoid phishing attacks – where scammers make fake versions of legitimate websites – by double checking that you are only clicking on official links.

Finally, keep in mind that blockchain networks are public, so transactions and wallet addresses can be viewed and monitored (using etherscan.io, for example).

Saying that they are public doesn't mean anyone can see the tokens you hold, as they would need to connect your personal information to a particular wallet or transaction. However, the fact that visibility is possible with the right kind of forensic analysis should tell you why it's important to be careful about with whom you share your wallet and transaction data.

Popular Wallets You Can Use

Below are a few examples of well-known hot and cold wallets that you may want to consider. Keep in mind that using multiple wallets is good security practice; therefore, as you progress in DeFi, you can and should use more than one of the examples provided.

MetaMask

MetaMask was launched in 2016 by ConsenSys as a web browser plug-in, and it later added mobile app functionality in 2020.

In October 2020, Consensys also added the Swaps functionality to Metamask, which allows users to trade crypto tokens directly in the wallet. In April 2021, ConsenSys reported that MetaMask had

5 million active monthly users, representing 5x growth during the previous six months.

MetaMask is compatible with ERC20 and ERC721 tokens, which are tokens designed for the Ethereum network. MetaMask is not compatible with Bitcoin, but users can access some other popular DeFi chains such as Binance Smart Chain (BSC) because these chains were specifically developed to be compatible with the Ethereum Virtual Machine (EVM) in order to easily migrate Ethereum DeFi users and developers.

DEFIYIELD has published a number of online tutorials that provide Metamask users with step-by-step instructions for how to add EVM-compliant chains, such as BSC, to their MetaMask wallets

Trust Wallet

Trust Wallet is Binance-owned and has become the most widely-used mobile DeFi wallet. It is multi-chain compatible (including Bitcoin) and also features a built-in Web3 browser, as well as staking functionality.

Trezor

Trezor, which means 'vault' in Czech, released the world's first hardware wallet and introduced the important seed recovery and passphrase protection (BIP39 and BIP44) processes.

Ledger

Ledger introduced the BOLOS operating system and was the first hardware wallet to incorporate two-factor authentication (2FA).

Game Theory

Game theory is a process of mathematical modelling used to study and predict human behavior based on the rational decisions each person would be expected to make in a "game" scenario. Game theory can play out in a wide range of contexts, including social interactions, business, war, biology, and many more.

It is certainly not exclusive to cryptocurrencies, but game theory does play an important role in various areas of the crypto market. For example, game theory influenced many aspects of the Bitcoin protocol's design to predict what might constitute the most secure network, if nefarious actors began to participate.

The use of game theory has influenced the design of virtually all cryptocurrencies and blockchain projects ever since, so it's always worth understanding this concept at a basic level. In terms of Yield Farming, game theory can be translated to:

- Always trying to understand the various entities involved in a project
- The incentives that are attracting entities to the project
- The rational or probable decisions entities might make based on these factors.

Incentives

IIncentives and incentive design play a very important role across blockchain and crypto technology. You should always have them in mind when assessing a new project or the entities involved in it.

Incentives are designed into systems to direct behaviors in a certain way. For example, Proof of Work (PoW) is the process used in the Bitcoin network to keep it as secure as possible, and the incentive that leads miners to expend energy in PoW consensus is the coins that miners receive as a reward.

Another example of incentives is how decentralized exchanges like Uniswap, or lending/borrowing projects like Compound, require liquidity to function. Therefore, they incentivize asset holders to lock up assets in a smart contract by rewarding them with an interest rate and governance tokens.

Different market participants have different objectives. Many of the best incentive designs in crypto networks or protocols manage to balance these objectives so that everyone benefits. That said, you should always take time to assess the incentives in any project you consider for Yield Farming, in order to identify incentives that are skewed towards one participant at the expense of the others. For example, with a fixed amount of reward tokens in a Farming pool, the more liquidity is locked, the less rewards-per-dollar-invested the participants receive. In other words, by investing more, you would be diluting those who already invested.

Memes

Your friends send you memes – funny pictures, videos, gifs, or phrases – all the time for a laugh, right? But memes are more than just a bit of fun when it comes to crypto markets. They actually play a sometimes surprisingly important role in how the market functions because they can have a greater effect on driving the success or failure of a project than you might expect.

For example, Elon Musk has heavily promoted Dogecoin and the memes that surround it through his Twitter account. As one of the richest people in the world, his attention to Dogecoin has had a dramatic effect on the asset's price.

This is just one simple example of the effect memes can have on crypto among too many other examples to count. However, it's worth looking at a couple more examples to demonstrate their power.

Bitcoin, as the original and most established cryptocurrency, has plenty of memes. "Digital gold," which has been mentioned already, is a powerful meme because it relates to the asset's store of value characteristic and the advantages it has over actual gold. "Hodl" (which is the intentional repetition of the misspelling of "hold" that first appeared in a post on bitcoin.org in 2013) is another important meme you should know. It relates to the idea that once you hold cryptocurrency, you should never sell it because regardless of volatility in the short-term, it is expected to be worth much more in the long run as cryptocurrencies rise and fiat currencies decline.

An important meme to understand in the world of DeFi is 'ETH is money.' This relates to the idea that, as Ethereum-based projects (particularly DeFi projects) continue to grow, ether is becoming synonymous with money in the same way that Bitcoin is synonymous with gold.

All of these examples are important narratives to understand because increasing numbers of participants are aligning with them every day, consciously and unconsciously. Subsequently, memes play an increasingly important role in how the markets move.

FUD (Fear, Uncertainty and Doubt)

With the memes comes the FUD--and there's almost as much of this as there are memes!. FUD covers conspiracy theory-style topics such as whether cryptocurrencies will be banned, how markets are manipulated by whales, and whether the whole idea of crypto is one big Ponzi scheme that is ready to collapse at any moment.

Essentially, the best way to deal with FUD concepts as a Yield Farmer is the same way you should deal with memes. You should know about them, do enough research to understand them, assess whether you think they are likely to have a big effect on the market, and plan your strategies accordingly.

Understanding memes and FUD as much as possible puts you in a strong position. You'll be able to take advantage of volatility when you sense that these important dynamics are weilding undue influence over market behavior.

Cycles

While many mainstream commentators describe cryptocurrency markets as volatile, this view is often skewed because they look at snapshots of the markets on days when things are particularly volatile. This viewpoint leads them to decide that cryptocurrency markets are worth their commentary.

However, seasoned cryptocurrency investors see far less volatility over the long term and generally agree that cryptocurrencies increase in value when viewed on a logarithmic scale (which is a way of compactly displaying numerical data over a very wide value range). They also recognize how, historically, the market has moved in roughly four-year cycles that are based on Bitcoin halvings or "halvenings" (i.e., pre-programmed events when the number of bitcoins a miner can receive as a reward for mining a new block is cut in half. This practice is to help keep Bitcoin's inflation rate in check).

This cycle may or may not continue in the future as Bitcoin dominance waxes and wanes, but what's really important for you to understand is where market participants generally agree we are in any cycle. This position matters to Yield Farming for a number of reasons, but some examples include:

- Paying lower fees during a bear market (as fewer transactions are occurring)

- Seeing greater asset returns from a less proactive strategy in a bull market (as everything rallies regardless)

The Most important DeFi Protocols

Hopefully you are starting to get excited about the opportunity that Yield Farming provides and are confident enough to get started! Learning is an ongoing process for everyone in this industry, and reading this book is a great start. Most important of all, however, is learning by doing – that is what will truly take your comprehension to the next level.

With that idea in mind, it's time to look at some of the best and most well-known DeFi projects that you can use to get started. You may well recognize the names of many projects because their profiles have been rapidly increasing over the last year. This section is intended to give you a better idea of the fundamentals behind them.

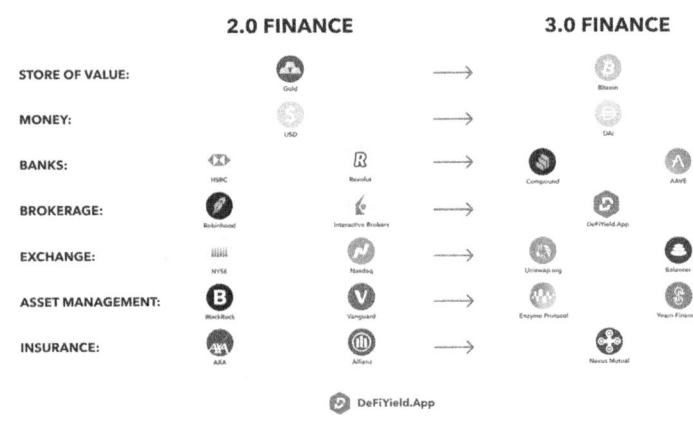

After looking at some specific projects, I'll go on to explain the important area of seigniorage coins, which is one of the most profitable areas of my strategy.

Lending and Borrowing Protocols

As with traditional finance, lending and borrowing is a key part of the decentralized financial system. Many of the earliest and most established DeFi protocols are focused on this area.

Many diverse DeFi protocols incorporate some element of lending and borrowing in their user services, even if it is not their core offering. Let's look at the key differences between lending and borrowing in traditional finance via a bank, like HSBC, and in decentralized finance via a protocol, like Compound or Aave, highlighted in the table on the next page:

MakerDAO

MakerDAO is one of the core protocols within DeFi.

This protocol offers a hybrid model of services for lending and borrowing that are built around the DAI stablecoin, which is one of the most trusted stablecoins the DeFi ecosystem uses.

Token holders can deposit various tokens into Maker vaults, where their deposits are used as collateral for loans. The collateral in the vaults is used to determine how many DAI tokens the owner of the collateral can mint and the applicable fees. DAI is a debt/loan the MakerDAO extends to a user and is secured by the tokens said user deposited to the vaults.

The most important point to remember about MakerDAO is that the DAI stablecoin it issues is decentralized, unlike other stablecoin issuers, such as Tether, where users simply wire fiat currency to a centralized entity. The entity that now controls their collateral mints the stablecoin. DAI is different; it's issued in a non-custodial fashion that involves only smart contract interactions.

Traditional Finance vs. Decentralized Finance

Lending and borrowing comparison

	Traditional 1.0		Decentralized 3.0	
Banks	HSBC	R Revolut	→  Compound	AAVE
Application time	**Several Weeks**		→ **A few minutes**	
	Even if you already have a bank account, it can take weeks for a credit department to agree to terms. Without a bank account in place, the whole process might take months.		To access a DeFi loan, all you need to do is deposit funds as collateral with a protocol like Aave or Compound. You can borrow what's needed in just a few clicks, as no middlemen are involved.	
Control of funds	**Custodial**		→ **Non-custodial**	
	Any funds lent are provided by the lender and held in an account in the client's name, which the bank allows the client to access.		The lending and borrowing takes place via decentralised smart contracts. The user holds funds in a wallet only they can access.	
Availability	**Limited and restricted**		→ **Trustless and borderless**	
	Only available to the borrowers who a credit department approves. This usually restricts access to the upper and middle classes within leading economies.		Totally open and available to anyone, anywhere who chooses DeFi. It is accessible to all races, religions, genders, and nationalities, without prejudice.	
Minimum amount	**Roughly $1,000**		→ **Just a few cents**	
	Traditional finance institutions have cut their costs and optimised their business models to suit large lending and borrowing, not ordinary people with small needs.		Because DeFi runs on smart contracts, human interaction costs are non-existent and users can access loans of any size to suit their needs.	

 DeFiYield.App

Compound Finance

Compound is a DeFi pioneer that enables anonymous lending and borrowing. CEO Robert Leshner and CTO Geoffrey Hayes founded it in 2017 to create a better crypto credit market.

Compound has introduced many innovations to the industry, including peer-to-peer lending, tokenized balances, and algorithmic interest rates. It has been highly rated by almost every Yield farmer as a result. It has also helped to make DeFi into a composable toolbox via integration with other DeFi projects. DeFi is often referred to as "Money Legos," since protocols can easily connect with each other in endless combinations, which makes the industry more flexible and enables better user returns.

Compound hasn't had completely smooth sailing, though, as its team has had to overcome many of the most significant issues to hit DeFi. These problems included the exponentially growing network/transaction fees (aka 'gas costs') that sometimes exceed the value of relatively small transactions and made the platform (and to be fair the platform's competitors on Ethereum Network) unattractive to anyone but the biggest investors. As an Ethereum-based protocol, it also didn't support non-Ethereum assets that were growing in popularity.

For these reasons, Compound has decided to develop Compound Chain, which is intended to be an autonomous distributed ledger that can support digital assets from a variety of different blockchains. This newly developed platform will support its own native token, called CASH, which is created through a borrowing process. Its holders and validators are rewarded with a compounded interest rate, which is currently 3%.

The token is designed to pay fees for transactions on Compound Chain. Users can borrow CASH after supplying any asset supported for collateral purposes and use it to pay fees.

When CASH is downloaded and held on peer blockchains, interest accumulates on Compound Chain by synchronizing with the interest index.

Currently, CASH is arbitrarily pegged to USD, but this arrangement can be adjusted in the future through governance. The governance of Compound Chain occurs through the initial Compound Governance system, according to which holders of the COMP governance token determine the network parameters through a voting process.

Asset Management Protocols

Protocols that manage digital assets within DeFi, such as Yearn Finance, play a similar role to those which asset managers like Black-Rock do in traditional finance.

In both cases, the role of these entities is to help the user invest their assets in a risk-adjusted manner to generate the appropriate Yield from these assets over time. The key difference is that asset management in DeFi is trustless, permissionless, and executed via smart contracts, rather than through middlemen as it is in traditional finance.

The key differences between the two approaches is summarized in the following table:

Yearn Finance

Yearn Finance is a project I began farming from the start, and it remains one of the main sources of my capital gains. Previously known as iEarn, it is a decentralized platform for asset management that provides a range of Yield Farming opportunities via liquidity provision, insuring DeFi risk and lending assets. However, its central product is Vaults, which allow users to maximize their Yield Farming returns through a combination of strategies.

Andre Cronje, who has since become one of the best-known people in Yield Farming, founded Yearn. He came up with the idea because he wanted to manage his own stablecoin portfolio in such a way that it would make it into his traditional bank savings account.

Traditional Finance vs. Decentralized Finance

Asset management comparison

	Traditional 1.0			Decentralized 3.0	
Asset Management	**B** BlackRock	**V** Vanguard	→	Enzyme Protocol	Yearn Finance
Application time	**Several Weeks** Even if you are applying to a bank where you have an account, approval from its compliance team could take several weeks.		→	**A few minutes** All it takes is a few clicks and a few minutes of your time to deposit the funds you control in protocols such as Yearn Finance.	
Control of funds	**Custodial** You hand over full control of your funds to an asset manager, who decides how and where to invest your money.		→	**Non-custodial** You choose which protocols to deposit your assets into and can decide based on fully transparent investment strategies.	
Availability	**Limited and restricted** Only the wealthiest citizens within leading economies have the funds required to access traditional asset managers.		→	**Trustless and borderless** Totally open and available to anyone. It is accessible to all races, religions, genders or nationalities, without prejudice.	
Minimum amount	**Roughly $1,000** Asset managers and hedge funds only want to work with clients who can deposit a minimum of several thousand dollars.		→	**Just a few cents** DeFi users can access asset management protocols like Yearn Finance with just a few dollars.	

DeFiYield.App

He also wanted to tackle what he believed was a big issue with how token economies worked, namely that playing with tokens sucked up energy and was generally a waste of capital. Therefore, he designed Yearn Finance as a Yield optimizer, mainly for stablecoins, in order to manage assets and automate profit maximization.

Yearn Finance's growth has been immense since it introduced its native YFI token, with the project's assets reaching over $400M within the first week of the token being introduced. At this point, the project drew a lot of attention through its interaction with Curve, the Ethereum-based exchange liquidity pool.

Users that provided liquidity to yPool and the YFI Balancer pool on Curve were eligible to claim the YFI token. The pools were developed to:

- Be used as Yield aggregators
- Automatically send staked funds to Compound and Aave for lending
- Receive additional returns from this operation

Apart from optimizing Yields, one of the most revolutionary approaches Yearn took was how it ensured the full decentralization of the project. It was the first DeFi project to introduce the concept of a "fair launch," with no pre-mine of tokens and no developer rewards. Instead, they took what is seen to be the most decentralized route. Instead of Cronje and his colleagues receiving tokens for building Yearn, they distributed its YFI token in a transparent and equitable manner.

This point is important because digital assets gain value when distribution, acknowledgement, and acceptance are balanced. Initially, it was settled that the total amount of tokens minted at the time would not be inflated and that 100% of these tokens would be distributed in Farming rewards.

In this respect, Yearn Finance introduced the very concept of Yield Farming.

While Andre Cronje initially had the exclusive right to mint tokens, he didn't use this right to his advantage. Instead, he transferred the right to mint tokens to nine multisig (multi-signature) owners, who were all active members of the DeFi community.

He notably left himself off this list. In accordance with the fair launch strategy, six signatures were required to submit the token minting, and Andre decided to not distribute any tokens to himself.

Such a favorable and community-oriented token distribution had never occurred in DeFi before. But with Yearn, all project participants got equal rights, equal risks, and were able to make decisions based on the same information.

This approach contrasts markedly with centralized crypto projects. In most cases, centralized crypto firms cooperate with influential and financially strong institutions such as venture capitalists, in order to help the project gain momentum. But Yearn was financed from the ground up with its fair launch. To many, this is why DeFi also represents an extremely important evolution in how startups and innovators are being funded.

The personality of Andre Cronje deserves special mention here, as he now has a strong influence on how the community perceives crypto events. He is a talented DeFi architect who has revolutionized Yield Farming. Andre also has a legal background and knowledge of various key areas of traditional finance, including banking and insurance.

His crypto involvement started in the ICO era, circa 2017, when he worked for large-scale blockchain projects such as Fusion and Fantom in technical advisory and leadership roles. In these roles, he reviewed the codebases of various ICOs, discovering their strengths and weaknesses. This experience eventually enabled him to develop the vision of an automated smart saving account that was fulfilled with Yearn Finance.

Multiple copycats were created very quickly following YFI's success, including YFII, YFIII, and many more. Some of these versions were obvious scams trying to ride the hype of the original project, which goes to show how significant it was.

Exchange Protocols

Traditional Finance vs. Decentralized Finance

Exchanges comparison

	Traditional 1.0			Decentralized 3.0	
Exchanges	NYSE	Nasdaq	→	Uniswap.org	Balancer
Listing Process	**Complicated and restricted** For an asset to be listed at the NYSE or Nasdaq, a huge amount of time, effort and money is required.		→	**Totally accessible** Anyone can list a token on Uniswap and create a market, no matter who they are or where they come from.	
Listing timeframe	**Many months** The complex legal and regulatory process means an initial public offering can take many months to navigate.		→	**A matter of minutes** Anyone can list a token on a decentralized exchange in minutes.	
Availability	**Limited to big corporations** Companies can only go public after a long and expensive legal process, which restricts it to an elite group of corporations.		→	**Open to any project** Any token can be listed, without restriction. It is then up to the market to decide whether the token is popular and worth trading.	

DeFiYield.App

Decentralized exchanges, including aggregators, liquidity protocols, and automated market makers (AMMs), have become the DeFi protocols with the most users, the most total value locked (TVL), and the most value exchanged.

For this reason, they are very important and increasingly abundant. Traditional finance exchanges such as the Nasdaq and the New York Stock Exchange also have key differences, which are summarized in the table above:

Bancor

Bancor is considered an important DeFi protocol because it was the first to introduce the concept of an AMM. (See the upcoming chapter, "How DeFi Protocols Earn Revenue" for a full explanation of AMMs.) While other protocols such as Uniswap have come to dominate the AMM space over time, the Bancor protocol continues to innovate.

In 2021, Bancor introduced the idea of single-sided exposure for liquidity pools as a solution to the problem of "impermanent loss." Impermanent loss is a frequently-heard term in DeFi – what follows is a brief explanation.

The problem of impermanent loss may occur when a token holder lends two separate tokens and locks up their assets in a DeFi protocol's smart contract in order to provide liquidity for exchange pairs of the two tokens.

If prices for the locked tokens shift too much in external markets, liquidity providers might experience a temporary loss on the value of tokens they have locked up. This loss becomes permanent if they remove their tokens from the liquidity pool at the wrong time.

Bancor has suggested a solution to the issue of impermanent loss in the form of single-sided exposure. This solution involves Bancor's BNT token providing the other side of a token pool's liquidity and thereby reducing the risk of impermanent loss. In addition, Bancor has suggested it will also insure liquidity providers against impermanent loss.However, you should remember that these single-sided exposure and insurance-related solutions are in their early days of development.

Uniswap

As mentioned, Uniswap followed Bancor into the AMM space. Since then, it has grown to become the largest and most well-known Decentralized Exchange (DEX) in the Ethereum DeFi ecosystem.

Uniswap is radically different from any sort of exchange that has been seen in the traditional finance world before. In many ways, it is a standard bearer for the whole DeFi ecosystem.

The key point that differentiates Uniswap from exchange competitors like Binance, Coinbase, and Kraken is decentralization. While these competitors all complete huge volumes of transactions every day, they require users to go through a centralized intermediary to do so, which means depositing funds into a centralized exchange's accounts and passing over control of your funds to them. It also means going through the Know-Your-Customer (KYC) process that these centralized exchanges require.

None of that is necessary with Uniswap. You can instantly exchange one asset for another without your funds going through an intermediary, meaning you are in full control of your assets right up until the moment you choose to exchange them. In this way, custody remains with you throughout – you act as your own bank.

To exchange digital assets via Uniswap, you need to store your assets in a digital crypto wallet. You can then send the desired funds to MetaMask, which is a popular cryptocurrency wallet that allows users to interact with Ethereum-based DeFi protocols like Uniswap. From there, it's a simple process of buying or selling tokens in an instant.

It's generally agreed that Uniswap has risen to the top of the DEX rankings because it is the easiest DeFi AMM to use. In addition, Uniswap users can earn passive income by depositing their tokens into fixed liquidity pools that contain 50% of one token and 50% of the other. Finally, it's worth noting that new protocols frequently use Uniswap to establish a liquid marketplace for their native token. Since Uniswap is widely used, doing so can help speed up growth of the new protocol's user base..

SushiSwap

SushiSwap is a decentralized cryptocurrency exchange and AMM created from a "fork" of the Uniswap protocol. Forks, or forking, is a temporary or permanent change that diverges a blockchain into different paths. Even though these two forks share the same genesis code, moving forward they exist as separate networks with different rules and governance.

SushiSwap has a fairly controversial history, due to a couple of high-profile incidents.The first involved what came to be referred to as a "vampire attack," wherein SushiSwap's initial launch incentives for its SUSHI token were designed to drain liquidity from Uniswap in order to boost SushiSwap's market position. (See more about vampire attacks in this book's section "Additional concepts to understand".)

The second event saw one of SushiSwap's main developers, the pseudonymous Chef Nomi, suddenly liquidate $14M of SUSHI tokens that were stored as a development fund. He decided to return the funds six days later. However, the overall effect of this unexpected event – which raised red flags that SushiSwap may be an exit scam – weakened the entire DeFi market for a period.

Credit goes to SushiSwap for surviving this rocky start and continuing to move forward. SushiSwap evolved from that point to become a community-driven protocol. It has retained a leading position in DeFi, mainly because of the attractive terms and incentives it has offered. Here are three highlights:

1. Sushiswap offered new terms for passive income. Liquidity providers on SushiSwap lock their funds into a pool and receive returns in the form of SUSHI. However, unlike Uniswap, the SUSHI tokens also allow liquidity providers to continue earning trading fees, paid in SUSHI, even when they unstack the deposited funds.

2. SushiSwap improved on an issue that Uniswap had when it came to diluting the rewards of smaller liquidity providers. Because staking larger amounts into Uniswap liquidity pools resulted in larger fees being paid to these providers, smaller liquidity providers became diluted as the total value of the Uniswap pools grew. SushiSwap solved this issue by distributing SUSHI tokens in a different way: they allowed early adopters to gain ten times more SUSHI than those who brought liquidity to the pools later on.

3. Sushiswap has also enabled limit orders. This is an important exchange feature that will attract traders and therefore should result in more fees for liquidity providers.

Curve Finance

Curve Finance is a decentralized exchange (DEX) and AMM designed to enable efficient token swaps. It focuses on stablecoins such as DAI, USDC, USDT, TUSD, BUSD, and sUSD and enables users to enjoy low impermanent losses and little slippage. Stablecoins are cryptocurrencies designed to peg their value to something external such as fiat currencies, other cryptos, or exchange-traded commodities.

Russian physicist Michael Egorov developed the idea for Curve in a whitepaper at the end of 2019 and launched it as a protocol in early 2020.

Even though Uniswap is the most well-known AMM, Curve Finance has managed to stand out because of the unique advantages it offers. First, Curve enabled lower transaction fees by swapping stablecoins directly with one another, rather than routing through the Ethereum blockchain and incurring the gas costs and slippage this method can cause (slippage is the difference between a trade's expected price and its actual price once it's executed – it's most prevalent when markets are volatile). Later on, Uniswap applied this same improvement in its own updated second version.

Next, Curve has managed to reduce slippage when swapping tokens. They achieved this feat through advanced mathematical formulas that define the relationship between token prices and their supply.

From there, Curve allowed liquidity providers to interact with Compound, enabling them to earn extra interest on top of fees by sharing liquidity. Therefore, users can increase their earnings without holding more volatile tokens. A similar interaction was made possible with Yearn, which allowed stablecoin holders to benefit from high interest through the automated rebalancing of the underlying tokens.

Several months after its initial success, Curve Finance issued its own governance token, Curve DAO (CRV). People who had invested in the project prior to the token launch were eligible to receive CRV in the token distribution. As a result, Yield farmers are attracted to Curve because they can receive Yield on their staked stablecoins and receive CRV rewards for providing liquidity.

Some pools offer even higher returns. These so-called incentivized pools include, for example, the sUSD pool that provides additional rewards in the form of Synthetix tokens (SNX).

The Yield Farming interest that is available from Curve pools fluctuates constantly, with the greatest return on stablecoins currently at around 5%. A process you can use to sers compare liquidity pools:

1. Gauge the total return for each one, by taking into account all additional interest paid in CRV and the pool's specific tokens.

2. Consider the high gas fees that come from interacting with Curve's smart contracts on Ethereum.

3. Decide how your frequency of withdrawing Yield could eat into any profit you gain.

Balancer

Balancer is another AMM worth understanding, mainly because of the unequal liquidity pools it enables.

Balancer's less-intuitive UX is generally thought to hold back its growth. Alternatives like Uniswap are easier to use. However, Balancer's "unequal liquidity pools" can provide good Yield opportunities for advanced users.

Unequal liquidity pools deviate from the starting 50:50 split that some AMMs use. Users might choose different correlations, such as 80:20, because they see an opportunity to generate more Yield from the assets they deposit. However, this should be considered an advanced strategy, as these Yield Farmers also expose themselves to increased impermanent loss risk.

dYdX

dYdX is a decentralized exchange built to meet the needs of traders who are used to centralized exchanges' high-quality user interface and feature-rich experience.

dYdX users benefit from derivatives, perpetual, and leveraged trading via a decentralized order book. This setup can be particularly useful if a trader wants to trade an asset that doesn't have a huge amount of liquidity on a decentralized market. dYdX users can create a derivative that doesn't require volume in the underlying asset and trade the risk instead.

dYdX Layer 2 Cross-margined Perpetuals are available on mainnet Ethereum with the integration of Starkware. With the L2 integration, dYdX aims at becoming a trustless, noncustodial version of Bitmex/Binance Futures.

Like many other protocols, dYdX offers lending and borrowing services as well.

Injective Protocol

Injective Protocol is another decentralized exchange that has emphasized an intuitive UI that appeals to everyone from new DeFi users to experienced traders. It operates as a cross-chain, interoperable relay chain, allowing users to trade spot and future derivatives.

0x

0x plays a significant role within DeFi. It is an open protocol that enables peer-to-peer asset exchange, making it useful to a number of other protocols when they create their own decentralized exchanges.

0x enables these protocols to build order books for their exchanges using the 0x protocol as an oracle for pricing. Oracles are verified data feeds such as price feeds for traditional financial assets, that can be used to price assets. (See more about them in this book's section "Other Important Protocols and Projects.")

As a result, 0x has become a major source of bid and ask prices for a variety of DEXes. In addition, DEX aggregator protocols use 0x to find the best price among a range of DEXes. Examples of this type of protocol include 1inch, Paraswap and Matcha. 0x built the last one itself.

PancakeSwap

PancakeSwap is a decentralized exchange that runs on Binance Smart Chain rather than Ethereum. It is also the largest project on Binance Smart Chain at the time of this writing, in terms of Total Value Locked (TVL).

It enables efficient swapping of BEP20 tokens, BEP20 being the token standard on Binance Smart Chain that extends and is compatible with Ethereum ERC-20. This swapping takes place via the AMM model and offers attractive Farming opportunities.

A decentralized exchange running on Binance Smart Chain has some key advantages, which include transactions that only cost a few cents, with transaction speeds of approximately 2,000 per second. Both metrics are much more attractive than their equivalents on Ethereum.

PancakeSwap offers Farming of its CAKE token, when users deposit and lock up liquidity pool (LP) tokens, known as FLIP tokens. LP tokens act like share certificates for the funds you have deposited, giving you the right to withdraw your funds according to your share of the whole liquidity pool. (See more about them in this book's section "Additional Concepts to Understand.")

Yield farmers can then also stake CAKE tokens to get additional rewards, which are paid in SYRUP tokens. The SYRUP token was developed as a governance and a lottery token. However, SYRUP tokens are discontinued at the time of this writing due to a smart contract flaw, with the project team migrating all distributed and future SYRUP tokens to CAKE-based pools.

Brokerage and Account Services

Traditional Finance vs. Decentralized Finance

Brokerage & account services

	Traditional 1.0			Decentralized 3.0
Banks	Robinhood Interactive Brokers		→	DeFiYield.App
Application time	**Several Weeks** Even if you already have a bank account, it can take weeks for a credit department to agree to terms. Without a bank account in place, the whole process might take months.		→	**A few minutes** To access a DeFi loan, all you need to do is deposit funds as collateral with a protocol like Aave or Compound. You can borrow what's needed in just a few clicks, as no middlemen are involved.
Control of funds	**Custodial** Any funds lent are provided by the lender and held in an account in the client's name, which the bank allows the client to access.		→	**Non-custodial** The lending and borrowing takes place via decentralised smart contracts. The user holds funds in a wallet only they can access.
Availability	**Limited and restricted** Only available to the borrowers who a credit department approves. This usually restricts access to the upper and middle classes within leading economies.		→	**Trustless and borderless** Totally open and available to anyone, anywhere who chooses DeFi. It is accessible to all races, religions, genders, and nationalities, without prejudice.
Minimum amount	**Roughly $1,000** Traditional finance institutions have cut their costs and optimised their business models to suit large lending and borrowing, not ordinary people with small needs.		→	**Just a few cents** Because DeFi runs on smart contracts, human interaction costs are non-existent and users can access loans of any size to suit their needs.

 DeFiYield.App

Brokerage and account services in DeFi involve managing and deploying assets across a variety of DeFi protocols and blockchain networks to generate Yield. The best brokerage and account services enable this service, while also protecting their users from scams by auditing DeFi smart contracts and only listing safe protocols for them to use.

A brokerage provider in traditional finance, such as Robinhood, and a DeFi brokerage protocol, such as DeFiYield, have many differences which are outlined in the table above.

DeFiYield

DEFIYIELD is a decentralized protocol for cross-chain asset management. It includes an all-in-one dashboard that allows users to manage their digital asset investments in one place, as well as a range of additional security products that protect users from scams.

CROSS-CHAIN ASSET MANAGEMENT DASHBOARD

The DeFiYield Dashboard allows users to manage their funds staked in liquidity pools and Yield Farming vaults. You can also use it to exchange tokens at the best rates and swap fiat currencies for cryptocurrencies.

Crucially, because DeFiYield is a cross-chain solution, it allows users to relocate funds across multiple blockchains. These blockchains currently include Ethereum, Binance Smart Chain, and Huobi ECO Chain, with new chains constantly being evaluated for potential inclusion.

One of DeFiYield's unique features is its presentation of precise calculations for Yield Farming rewards. The platform allows users to see detailed metrics about their portfolio's performance, including:

- P&L chart with hourly, daily, monthly, and yearly overview

- P&L value for selected timeframe
- Accrued expenses
- Earned value
- Gas costs
- Impermanent loss
- Claimable rewards
- Fees earned

AIn addition to helping users track investments, DeFiYield also makes it easier to develop DeFi investment strategies. The platform provides detailed information about DeFi protocols and in-depth audits of the smart contracts they use.

These are just some of the DeFiYield tools that help users deposit their funds in the safest DeFi protocols, while generating the maximum Yield. Please visit us at DeFiYield to see the latest ways in which we're improving DeFi.

Derivative Protocols

Derivatives are financial instruments that derive their value from an underlying asset. Examples from the traditional finance world include futures, options, and credit default swaps. In the case of DeFi, this underlying asset might be a digital or traditional asset.

As a result, some of the best-known derivative protocols in DeFi were established to enable the trading of products from traditional finance by "wrapping" them in a digital asset derivative. Wrapping in this context means creating compatibility with a particular blockchain, like Ethereum.

Synthetix

Synthetix is a very important DeFi project that may well play a significant role in the industry for years to come. It provides what's known as a synthetic market for every asset imaginable.

Synthetic assets replicate other assets by using smart contract-based derivatives that derive value from an underlying asset. These underlying assets could include commodities, fiat or crypto currencies, stocks, interest rates, bonds, indexes, and more. Stablecoins, which peg their value to fiat or crypto currencies, are an example of a synthetic asset.

The platform, which was founded by Kain Warwick, was launched in December 2018. It is a borderless and limitless marketplace that essentially wraps every asset into something that can be traded. This is a welcome development because trading certain assets can be difficult for some investors. For example, you might want to trade gold, cobalt, or Tesla stocks but be restricted from doing so because of where you live in the world, or because those markets are not open to anyone but specialist investors, among other reasons.

In Synthetix, however, these restrictions go away. On this platform, you can trade a synthetic derivative that represents the underlying asset. From there, you can implement your chosen strategy to take advantage of the price changes you expect, without ever having to trade the actual underlying asset. Being able to trade via Synthetics opens up numerous benefits for all participants that reduce friction and costs, while encouraging market innovation.

Synthetix also allows traders to use leverage in their trades. Leverage is borrowed funds that increase a user's trade position beyond their available cash balance, which can amplify profits as well as losses. These features combine to make it a vast derivative liquidity project, one that may well expand in size and influence.

Also notable is Synthetix' "Spartan Council, "which is a delegated council with seven seats that was established in December 2020 to govern the Synthetix protocol. It is an example of one of the many approaches to protocol governance, which aim for varying ratios of centralization to decentralization.

Other Important Protocols and Projects

DeFi is only in its early days of development, but even at this early stage, some potentially huge and transformational projects are being developed right now.

The following examples are projects you should definitely be aware of as you start your Yield Farming journey, as they are not only important within this immature industry right now but could also grow into huge and truly fundamental projects in the future.

The Graph

The Graph is an indexing protocol for querying decentralized networks. It has been labelled the Google of DeFi, and more widely, Web3. Yaniv Tal and Brandon Ramirez founded it in 2018, and the mainnet was launched in December 2020.

The Graph solves the problem of searching through the huge amounts of data available on public blockchain networks by doing so in a fast, efficient, and decentralized way. You may be aware of blockchain analytics services that already search and index blockchain data. However, most of these are centralized services that extract the publicly available information, index and store it on their own databases, and then make it available to others (usually for a fee).

The Graph is different because it enables this indexing of information in a totally decentralized way, which is why most DeFi projects use The Graph to display data about blockchain networks that users need to make financial decisions.

This protocol is becoming the standard for big data analysis within DeFi because it is a trustless and open-sourced way of figuring out the best data source. This process is enabled within The Graph network by incentivizing validators, indexers, and curators to work in tandem to search for and organise data from blockchain networks.

It is a hugely significant service that is worth knowing about now, as it will likely be used by most Ethereum-based projects and probably also across many other smart contract platforms.

Oracles

While The Graph is an example of a protocol that allows DeFi projects to use the data from public blockchain networks to enrich the services they offer their users, these same projects may also need to use data that comes from other sources.

In DeFi (and Web 3.0 more generally), the best way of accomplishing this objective is through oracles. Essentially, oracles are verified data feeds (such as price feeds for traditional financial assets that can be used to price synthetic derivatives.

Trustless DeFi is enabled by trustless oracles, and truly decentralized applications will aim to use decentralized oracles. These networks act as the antennae for data that is relevant to DeFi, collecting it from all sorts of sources and feeding it through to the projects that need it.

Oracles can help DeFi projects avoid the disruption that might be caused by an asset's price crashing on a single exchange, as prices gathered from multiple decentralized oracles would mitigate any damage. Not all DeFi projects use decentralized oracles. Compound's use of Coinbase price data feeds is a well-known example of a closed data source.

Chainlink

Chainlink is the most well-known decentralized oracle network, with a market cap that puts it in or around the top 10 cryptocurrencies. It was first conceived as far back as 2014 by CEO Sergey Naxarov, who raised funds via an ICO in 2017 and went live with its mainnet in June 2019.

Chainlink is made up of a network of decentralized nodes that connect off-chain data sources to smart contracts on the blockchain. It is used by a whole range of DeFi protocols for this reason, but it is also used by a whole range of other decentralized applications.

Apart from the fact that it has been around for a long time, Chainlink's growth has also benefited from the support of LINK Marines, the coin's adopters who have a strong presence across social media.

Decentralized Insurance

Decentralized insurance protocols are a growing niche within decentralized finance, but they currently relate to insurance coverage for a set of specific risks, rather than mirroring the wide range of events that can be insured in traditional markets.

For example, one of the key decentralized insurance products that is available covers breaches or exploits of smart contracts. Nexus Mutual and other decentralized insurance protocols offer coverage for this type of incident.

One key similarity with the traditional insurance world is that the claims these protocols pay out for usually involve an element of discretion. For Nexus Mutual, the governance of these decisions revolves around holders of the native token, and these participants decide to vote for or against a claim.

Seigniorage coins

Seigniorage coins are algorithmic stablecoins that form the basis of a number of projects, which means their value is not collateralized with any asset and is instead adjusted algorithmically through certain supply dynamics.

One of the main reasons they are so important is because they may provide a solution to the problems of using cryptocurrencies as a medium of exchange

Empty Set Dollar

Mervyn Chng, Co-Founder of stakewithus first introduced Empty Set Dollar. The project's ESD token was designed to become the reserve currency of DeFi, and you need to purchase ESD tokens for bonding to get started.

From here, you can generate Yield by taking advantage of the expansion and contraction cycles that the token goes through. The expansion cycle occurs when the price of ESD is above the $1 peg and the supply of ESD tokens is being raised.

Dynamic Set Dollar

Dynamic Set Dollar (DSD) is very similar to ESD, but it utilizes a more reactive mechanism of supply adjustments and includes improved terms for users. It's important to point out that DSD is not based on a rebase system, so holders won't experience changes in the token balance within their wallet. Instead, the price stability is reached by giving holders a financial incentive to sell or burn tokens, which is referred to as Voluntary Elastic Supply.

When the price of DSD rises above the $1 peg, the protocol activates the expansion phase and new DSD tokens are minted. The token supply can increase by a maximum of 10% every two hours, with the total expansion limited to 35%. These newly-minted tokens are then distributed to reward DAO stakers and liquidity providers..

TThe seigniorage and algorithmic stablecoin opportunity peaked around December 2020, after which time some protocol values have dipped as much as 90%. Surfing the token supply cycles of seigniorage coins provided high and stable incomes for a period, and since the market is still young, some imperfections should be expected.

One of the protocols that has emerged from the hype cycle with a positive image is Frax, which did not lose its peg even after several tests. This segment of DeFi is working on perfecting its toenomics and is worth watching, as it might catch on again in the future.

How DeFi Protocols Earn Revenue

Before we dive into how individual farmers can profit from opportunities that DeFi projects provide, let's examine how these DeFi projects earn their revenue.

In DeFi, projects can employ many different business models. Innovation occurs at breakneck speed in this industry. New projects can employ and integrate elements from different models in order to earn revenue, in endlessly varying combinations – the composability or "money legos" we discussed earlier.

To get started with Yield Farming, however, you only really need to understand the main DeFi protocol revenue models. We explain them below.

Type of Revenue	Type of protocol	Examples
Credit margin The difference between rates for borrowing and lending.	Lending and borrowing.	Aave Compound Cream Venus
Asset rehypothecation Using spare or under-utilized assets to generate yield.	Lending and borrowing, exchanges and others.	Celsius yEarn ••• others
Fees Either service fees or additional gas charges.	Asset management, aggregators and relayers.	yEarn (2% Management, 20% Performance fees on Vaults) Pickle (0.5% exit, 3% subsidized gas fees on Jars/Vaults) Harvest 1inch Paraswap
Exchange spreads Finding arbitrage opportunities between exchanges.	Aggregators.	Kyberswap
Dev Rewards Benefitting from a price increase in the native token.	Almost all DeFi projects.	1inch token (1INCH) allocations: • 22.5% core team and future employees; • 19.5% to investors and shareholders.

DeFiYield.App

DeFi Protocol Revenue Streams Part 2

Type of Revenue	Type of protocol	Examples
Dev Rewards Benefitting from a price increase in the native token.	Almost all DeFi projects.	Harvest Finance token (FARM) allocations: • 10% of the FARM tokens will vest to the Operational Treasury; • 20% of the FARM tokens will vest to the Development Team.
Yield Farming Early adoption of the protocol's incentive mechanisms.	Used by almost every project with farming tools but not always made public.	As an example, a project team providing liquidity at an early stage using its funds from development reserve or otherwise, would have high chances to capital gains in the case of an increase in the project token price.

DeFiYield.App

But first, dev rewards.

Before looking at the specifics, let's discuss the important concept of dev rewards.

Here's a good starting point: each DeFi protocol operates as its own central bank and digital asset issuer. The majority of projects function this way during initial coin offerings (ICOs) or initial exchange offerings (IEOs) to allocate a specific portion of tokens towards internal funding. This allocation to developers is usually referred to as dev rewards, and it represents financing required for ongoing development.

Why does this system matter? Because even though a protocol's ecosystem might be considered sufficiently decentralized at an early stage, the initial brainpower and development capacity come from a centralized entity.

Understandably, this entity needs to be rewarded for the significant value it provides early on, and dev rewards are the solution. These rewards are normally structured to avoid any substantial downward pressure on the native token's price that otherwise might occur if the team was able to sell its dev rewards without restrictions.

Following are the primary ways that DeFi protocols earn revenue:

Here are the specific ways we see these mechanisms play out in DeFi.

Credit Monetization

Well-known examples of projects in this category include Compound, Aave, Cream, and Venus. Think of them as decentralizing the way traditional banks use deposits and loans to generate revenue.

In a credit monetization model:

- A project attracts liquidity from the market by providing interest rates on the deposits made.

- These rates may be fixed or variable.

- The liquidity that has been attracted from lenders is then provided to borrowers, with a margin added to deposit rates.

- These loans are also available at fixed and variable rates, with the fixed rates normally higher than the variable ones.

An additional feature of DeFi credit monetization projects that's different from traditional banks is that they usually incentivize customers to deposit or borrow funds. They do this by distributing rewards to users in the form of platform tokens.

Sometimes a particular asset has excessive liquidity because more funds have been lent by depositors than have been loaned to borrowers. That's when projects might choose to put these assets to work in a different way.

For example, they might lend these deposits to other projects, in a process that mirrors interbank (bank-to-bank) loans in traditional finance. Alternatively, they might invest funds in automated asset management projects, which are detailed below. In addition, whenever a project chooses to distribute a token and the token becomes freely tradeable, the project might also sell tokens to generate additional revenue. However, this decision will depend on how the token was distributed and its utility characteristics.

Automated Market Maker (AMMs)

The Automated Market Maker (AMM) market started initially with the Bancor Network. Other well-known examples of platforms in this category include Uniswap, Balancer, Curve, and SushiSwap.

Think of AMMs as an open-air marketplace. Essentially, anyone can use these projects to set up shop in a trading market (except for Curve among the projects mentioned above).

An AMM user would:

- Set up a trading market to facilitate the exchange of any tokens that are acceptable to the network.
- Earn revenue on the trading fees.
- Set up a trading market to connect and exchange one token for another, provided there is sufficient liquidity.

The host protocol earns revenue by charging fees for trading. It may also introduce wider spreads between the buying and selling prices of certain token pairs and subsequently benefit from arbitrage opportunities.

As with other DeFi projects, these AMM projects may also choose to distribute a native token. The platform might retain that token, or sell it for profit on the open market at times of price appreciation.

Automated Asset Management

Well-known examples of projects in this category include yEarn, Pickle, and Harvest.

Think of these projects as asset managers in traditional finance. The service they provide is based around routing customer funds to various parts of the DeFi market. Then they can take advantage of various DeFi instruments and achieve the highest possible Yield.

These projects usually offer single asset vaults, each one holding only USDC or DAI, for example, or a specific liquidity pool share token. They use these to collect customer funds and accumulate revenues; for instance by selling rewards/incentives. Customers can then redeem these revenues in return for paying a fee to the project that provided the vault.

These projects attract users and generate revenue by providing the most profitable strategies across volatile markets, in parallel with the cheapest transaction costs. The cost-effectiveness of the platform is particularly important if users are seeking Yield as part of a strategy that involves multi-layer transactions because these multi-layer interactions with multiple smart contracts can potentially generate a lot of network fees. Automated asset management projects try to reduce these costs and generate revenue for themselves via the transaction savings they enable.

Once again, these projects can also generate additional income from a native token. The platform may partially retain it or sell it for profit on the open market at times of price appreciation..

Aggregators, Routers & Relayers

Well-known examples of aggregator, router, and relayer platforms include 1inch, Paraswap, and Matcha.

Their business model is built around finding and providing the best exchange rates for traders, which they do by:

- Integrating with and connecting to multiple liquidity sources

- Routing buy and sell orders

- Finding the optimal balance of FX rate and network fees

Some of these projects also use off-chain order book management to substantially reduce the related network fees, which can jump to extremely high levels.

Projects can also use "slippage surplus" to generate revenue, which is the case with 1inch. In this model, the platform generates revenue by collecting the positive difference between the order price when the transaction was confirmed and the actual settlement price. These platforms can also generate revenue from a native token. The platform may partially retain this native token or sell it for profit on the open market.

Additional Concepts to Understand

Before you take your first steps into Yield Farming, it's worth detailing some related concepts that will help you to understand how the industry works and some of the dangers that exist within it.

Decentralized Governance and DAOs

One of the most important benefits of decentralized finance is that you are able to take advantage of the decentralized governance that DeFi projects offer. As mentioned previously, decentralization is at the heart of the innovation that cryptocurrencies and block-chain technology provide.

Traditional Governance vs. Decentralized Governance

Limited Company vs Decentralized Autonomous Organisation (DAO)

	Centralized	Decentralized
Decision Making	**Limited** Directors and management only.	**Unlimited** Any stakeholder can have their say.
Proposing changes	**Restricted** Restricted to those with executive powers as defined by a legal structure.	**Open** Open to any community member within a truly decentralized structure.
Quorum and approval thresholds	**Fixed in legal documents** The legal documents define the minimum thresholds for votes to be valid.	**Defined by smart contract** This can remain as initially deployed or adjusted via community vote.
Influence on decisions	**Controlled by elites** Normally limited to majority shareholders and management.	**Available to anyone** All community members are listened to as defi protocols are open to innovation.
Barriers to entry	**High difficulty** Specific legal procedures cover how members can withdraw, depending on the entity setup.	**Easy access** Any stakeholder can withdraw at any time by disposing of governance tokens.
Transferability	**Complicated** Specific procedures exist for the transferring of rights, depending on the entity setup.	**Simple** Usually any stakeholder can freely transfer their governance tokens to any other person or wallet.
Understanding dilution	**Effort intensive** It may require substantial effort and legal costs to fully understand how one's influence on decision making can be reduced.	**Clear and transparent** By evaluating smart contracts, one can understand any perspective dilution scenarios or related risks.

DeFiYield.App

In its truest form, decentralized governance is embodied by a Decentralized Autonomous Organization or DAO, which is a totally new form of organizational structure enabled by blockchain technology. Unlike a limited company, which exists within the legal frameworks of a particular state, a DAO exists only on the internet. The rules that govern a DAO are encoded in a series of smart contracts, in much the same way the rules that govern a limited company are written down in legal documents.

However, DAOs can be much more open, transparent, and easy for anyone in the world to interact with or take part in.

The specific benefits of decentralized governance within a DAO, as compared to centralized governance in a limited company, can be seen in the table.

How DeFi Uses Decentralized Governance and DAOs

Just as DeFi is an emerging industry, so is decentralized governance an emerging concept. Therefore, not all DeFi protocols can be said to embrace fully decentralized governance. While full decentralization should be any protocol's ultimate goal, individual DeFi protocols have adopted their own approach for various reasons.

Founder Control: The least decentralized projects have a similar governance structure to private companies, with founders guiding the project strategy, controlling the execution of the technical roadmap, and 'DeFining' the project's future.

Some projects will claim that they lean towards this form of governance temporarily because they are at an early stage, and the mechanics required for the project to function correctly are not launched yet.

This can be a reasonable position, but unfortunately some projects fail to prove they are moving towards decentralization by making the necessary code changes in the protocol. For example, they will not design steps to transfer governance to or share governance with users, so we flag this lack of open governance to the community.

Council Model: This approach is sometimes used by immature projects. It involves selecting a group of experts to help make decisions about the product, roadmap, and any issues that must be resolved. Councils are usually made up of core developers and established crypto founders such as Andre Cronje or Stani Kulechov. This partnership style approach is usually in high demand because of the industry influence these individuals wield.

Representative Democracy: Users are able to elect individuals to represent them, and this group of representatives is assigned to making decisions concerning project development on the users' behalf.

Full Decentralization: TThis is what open governance looks like, and it is something we have never seen before in traditional finance. This approach is enabled by governance tokens, with projects distributing governance tokens to users so they are put in direct control of a project's future. A project may choose to use a Decentralized Autonomous Organization (DAO) platform such as Aragon to manage this process.

The primary goal of governance tokens within DeFi is to give project users the right to influence strategic decisions about how the project develops and how to solve any issues. Governance token holders are able to influence the direction of the project by:

- Proposing a change and initiating a vote to decide whether it goes ahead

- Voting for or against a change that they or another user has proposed

The growing demand for governance tokens indicates how crypto market participants want to take control of how DeFi projects use their assets. Furthermore, as the weight of a user's vote is directly correlated with the amount of governance tokens they hold or stake, many people believe this is a good reason to acquire as many governance tokens as they can.

This innovative approach to governance has definitely raised the standards of how all crypto projects are designed and run.

	DELAWARE, LLC	ETHEREUM, DAO
Structure	Legal shares	Token share
Medium	Analog	Digital
Database	Registered to a Nation State	Registered to the Internet
Access Control	Nation State Identity (SSN)	Private Key
Requirements	Citizenship or U.S. Status	Internet connection
Financial System	Traditional Finance	Decentralized Finance
Bank Account	BOA, JPMorgan, WellsFargo	Ethereum Address
Registration Costs	$90 one-time +$300 annual	$20 one-time gas fee
Credit	Robust credit system	Not currently available
Protocol Taxes	State & Federal Taxes (20 to 40% of profits)	None
Jurisdiction	United States	Global
System Cost	Entire U.S. Government (Double digit trillions annually)	Ethereum Protocol (Single digital billions annually)

BANKLESS

When governance tokens don't work: It's worth noting that governance tokens are not a panacea for all issues related to governance, and they can lead to undesirable consequences.

For example, if governance rights are tokenized but no vesting period is put in place for the tokens, a malicious founder could dump their tokens onto the open market, causing a supply shock that undermines the price of the token as well as the project's credibility.

Another potential issue might arise if an already well-established project uses its position to acquire a significant portion of a new project's governance token, resulting in parts of the DeFi ecosystem becoming centralized in the hands of the larger project's token holders.

Benefits of Decentralized Governance for DeFi Users

To understand how an individual defi user can benefit from decentralized governance, let's refer to the example of a bank account in traditional finance. Even if you are a citizen within one of the world's leading economies and don't fear government seizure of your funds, you should look at the money sitting in your bank account and consider whether it might be put to better use in DeFi for several reasons. First, consider Yields. Interest rates in major fiat economies are at historic lows and likely to remain so for the foreseeable future. You could receive an interest rate of under 1% in a traditional bank account or at least 10% in DeFi.

Furthermore, if you are interested in seeking Yield on your investments, DeFi provides far greater potential for you to take control of that process than is possible in traditional finance because of decentralized governance and DAOs. If, for example, you decided to seek better Yield than a standard bank account provides and opened your funds up to the bank's wealth management department, you might achieve better Yields (although it's likely they still won't be as good as in DeFi).

But what happens in this scenario if the 'advice' you receive isn't very good? Can you go to the wealth manager and start to dictate terms? Maybe that's possible if you're investing millions, but not if you're the average investor.

With DeFi, if you don't think a project is offering the best investment opportunities and strategies, you can change them by using your governance tokens to vote for the ones you like. This is the real power of open and decentralized governance. .

Stablecoins

Stablecoin Categories

Type	Description	Examples
Fiat-backed	An Ethereum stablecoin can represent a U.S. dollar, with each token issued backed by a corresponding U.S. dollar in a treasury.	USDC USDT
Crypto collateralized	An Ethereum stablecoin can be issued when collateralized by other digital assets like ETH, BAT, or USDC.	DAI
Interest-bearing stablecoin	An Ethereum token can be created to represent a stablecoin deposit earning interest, also known as an interest-bearing stablecoin.	cUSDC aUSDC aUSDT
Synthetic	An Ethereum token can be synthetic, introduced by synthetix where sUSD is backed by SNX holders, who are rewarded for providing collateral and stability with fees generated by Synth transactions.	sUSD
Algorithmic	An Ethereum token can be programmed to optimize in search of the highest yield opportunities, or have its treasury managed through the minting and burning of existing supply.	AMPL yUSDC

Source: Consensys   DeFiYield.App

Stablecoins are tokens designed to maintain a stable price that is pegged to another asset. In most cases, the asset is the US dollar, but some stablecoins track other fiat currencies as well as gold and stock market indices.

In recent years, stablecoins have become much more prominent in crypto, mainly because they allow traders and investors to monitor and denominate gains and losses in a currency that's value has remained far more stable over time than most cryptocurrencies have.

As a result, stablecoins have replaced bitcoin and ether as the primary medium of exchange for crypto trading pairs. They have also become a core component of DeFi, with the supply of stablecoins increasing in line with the rise of DeFi. According to Consensys, stablecoin total supply on Ethereum increased almost seven times over, from $5.5 billion in Q1 2020 to $37.4 billion in Q1 2021.

Different Types of Stablecoin

As mentioned, the most common peg used in stablecoins is the US dollar. Different stablecoin projects use different mechanisms for maintaining this peg and experience different levels of success in doing so.

Some stablecoins support a huge amount of transactional trading while retaining a value that is extremely close to the $1 peg. However, others completely fail to retain this peg as a result of poor design or insufficient dollar reserves.

To use stablecoins successfully in DeFi, it is therefore crucial that you understand how these mechanisms work and whether the $1 peg stability is likely to be maintained.

FIAT-BACKED STABLECOINS

Fiat-backed stablecoins are generally considered to be the most reliable mechanism for retaining a peg, but this reliability comes at the expense of decentralization. Every stablecoin issued is backed

1:1 by a corresponding dollar deposited in a bank account controlled by the entity that mints the stablecoin.

Tether USDT is the dominant stablecoin of this kind, with a market size of $52 billion as of Q2 2021. It is also the most liquid and heavily-traded token among all cryptocurrencies. However, the true extent of the dollar reserves backing USDT has been questioned, with the New York State Attorney General concluding in February 2021 that the stablecoin was not fully backed.

USDC is the second-largest fiat-pegged stablecoin and is owned by the Coinbase exchange and Circle Inc., under the CENTRE consortium. USDC dollar reserves are regularly audited and publicly reported. In 2021, Visa announced it will allow for transaction settlement with USDC on Ethereum, representing a giant leap towards mainstream adoption.

It is important to note that all major centralized stablecoin issuers retain the power to blacklist wallet addresses and have blocked wallets from using the stablecoin in the past at the request of law enforcement.

CRYPTO-COLLATERALIZED STABLECOINS

These stablecoins are backed by the collateral of other digital assets.

DAI is the most well-known example of crypto-collateralized stablecoins, and it was introduced in 2017 by the MakerDAO protocol. As per the rules of the MakerDAO smart contracts, DAI is backed by a basket of tokens, which includes ETH, LINK, YFI, UNI, and fiat-backed stablecoins like USDC.

These stablecoins are usually highly over-collateralized, meaning the collateral value of the MakerDAO crypto reserves far exceeds the value of issued DAI. Unlike USDT and USDC, no central authority is able to blacklist DAI wallets.

SYNTHETIC STABLECOINS

This category specifically refers to sUSD, a US dollar-pegged token introduced by Synthetix and backed by SNX holders. Platform users can mint sUSD tokens by staking SNX tokens and trading them against other synthetic assets.

The sUSD pegging mechanism is complex, but it essentially correlates the supply of sUSD with demand for the Synthetix platform. As with DAI, it is operated by smart contracts and cannot be centrally determined or blacklisted.

INTEREST-BEARING STABLECOINS

Examples include cUSDC or aUSDC, which represent USDC deposited in the Compound or Aave protocols respectively, in order to earn interest from lending. This category includes tokens with complex algorithmic components such as yUSDC, which represents USDC deposited in the Yearn protocol and programmed to continuously reallocate assets to optimize yield.

ALGORITHMIC STABLECOINS

Algorithmic stablecoins are a broad category of stablecoins that are not backed by an underlying asset. Instead, they aim to maintain a peg through complex mechanisms of token minting and burning that are based on game theory.

Although algorithmic stablecoins may seem appealing because they can be established without the need for a collateral reserve, none of them have proven successful over the long term.

Seigniorage tokens like ESD, DSD, and BAC have tended to lose their peg within weeks. Elastic supply algorithmic tokens like

AMPL have managed to oscillate around their intended peg but have also suffered huge volatility.

Fractional-algorithmic stablecoins like FRAX have been relatively successful in maintaining their peg. However, this model is still partially dollar collateralized and therefore can't be labelled as a truly algorithmic stablecoin, even though it does still expose holders to algorithmic risk.

Token Standards

Token Standards

	ERC-20	ERC-721	ERC-1155
Proposed	November 2015	January 2018	June 2018
Officially Recognized	September 2017	June 2018	June 2019
What it does	Defines a common list of rules that all fungible Ethereum tokens should follow rules that all fungible Ethereum tokens should follow.	Allows the implementation of non-fungible assets within a smart contract.	Allows the implementation of various fungible tokens, non-fungible tokens, and semi-fungible tokens in a smart contract.
Token Creation	Create assets that have value and can be sent and received.	Create only one token in a single contract.	Create multiple tokens in a single contract.
Example	DAI, ETH, UNI	CryptoPunk, Sorare, Axie Infinity	Euler Beats

Source: Consensys   DeFiYield.App

Token standards are the rules defining a token's properties and how it interacts with other tokens. The standards are important because they ensure compatibility, so independently-issued tokens and smart contracts can interact consistently and predictably.

The most common token standards on the Ethereum network are ERC-20 and ERC-721.

ERC-20

This is the most common standard and is the one used by the most well-known tokens on the Ethereum network, including USDT, DAI, UNI, SNX, LINK, and YFI. ERC-20 provides a standard interface for fungible tokens, meaning the same sort of ERC-20 tokens are equally exchangeable with one another (i.e., one DAI token is exchangeable with another DAI token). Core DeFi tasks such as staking and governance follow the ERC-20 standard.

ERC-721

ERC-721 is the standard for non-fungible tokens (NFTs), which are unique digital assets that are not equally exchangeable with one another. Digital art in the form of NFTs are the most well-known examples of ERC-721 tokens, but the standard can be adopted for many other use cases. ERC-721 is also used for collectibles like trading cards, for characters or costumes in gaming, and also to represent real-world assets like lottery tickets or seats at events. Some well-known examples of ERC-721 tokens are Hashmasks, CryptoPunks, and Axie Infinity.

ERC-1155

This standard enables the creation of assets in a smart contract, including fungible, non-fungible and semi-fungible tokens. It is sometimes known as a multi-token because it allows the creation of multiple tokens within the same contract. The main benefits of this standard are to reduce the fragmentation of tokens and to ensure better integration of fungible and non-fungible tokens, which are normally incompatible.

Liquidity Pool (LP) Tokens

As mentioned, many DeFi projects want to attract liquidity from cryptocurrency holders in order to enable the financial transactions at the heart of their business model. Therefore, when you start Yield Farming, you will begin by depositing funds into liquidity pools in order to generate Yield.

Liquidity pool (LP) tokens act like share certificates for the funds you have deposited, giving you the right to withdraw your funds according to your share of the whole liquidity pool. This can be a disconcerting process when you do it for the first time, as you will confirm the deposit of funds and see your account has been debited for this amount. What is not immediately clear, though, is what you hold in return for this deposit, which is where LP tokens come in, as these are included in the same transaction.

In order to see the LP tokens you hold, and therefore what share of the total liquidity pool you can redeem, you will need to inspect the transaction with a blockchain explorer. When you do, you will see the amount debited from your account and the LP tokens you hold. For example, if you were depositing into a Uniswap liquidity pool, you would see UNI LP tokens that represent your share of the liquidity pool and therefore the proportion of trading fees from this liquidity pool to which you are entitled.

Most of the time, you can use these LP tokens to withdraw your funds whenever you want. However, some projects may limit withdrawals or add a fee for withdrawing funds outside of certain set parameters. Finally, it's worth remembering that each pool's tokens are unique, even if the assets within the pools are the same. There-fore, you couldn't exchange Uniswap LP tokens for SushiSwap LP tokens, even if both tokens represented a share of an underlying ETH: USDC liquidity pool.

Finally, it's worth noting that DeFiYield allows users to trade their LP tokens.

Vampire Attacks

A vampire attack is specifically designed to drain liquidity from a DeFi project, and a rival project usually engineers it in order to at-tract users during the early stages of development. These kinds of attacks are possible because most DeFi protocols are developed as open source and permissionless projects.

While some projects try to attract users by offering better services, some well known DeFi projects have used vampire attacks where they simply replicated the functionality of a competitor and at-tracted its users by offering better Yield Farming terms.

Well-known examples include SushiSwap, which established itself as an Ethereum-based DeFi project by attacking Uniswap, and PancakeSwap, which made a similar manoeuver by attracting DeFi users on to Binance Smart Chain and away from Ethereum when the network's fees were very high.

DeFiYield Farmers need to be aware of vampire attacks because they can provide great opportunities that may only be short-term, if the terms that enable the attack are changed.

Black Swan Events

You may recognize the notion of a black swan event from your understanding of traditional finance. The metaphor is used to describe an unexpected and often catastrophic event that few people predicted.

Nassim Taleb developed the theory to explain the significant role that unexpected events have played in history. Essentially, the metaphor was used because black swans were not thought to exist and are often used to describe situations where humans' psychological biases make them unable to see rare events.

In the context of DeFi, a black swan event occurred on March 12, 2020, when the price of Bitcoin crashed by roughly 50%. You need to understand the potential harm that a black swan event can cause and always ensure you have a margin of safety that will protect you from them, at least to some extent. Degens, or high-risk traders and investors who operate in crypto markets with little or no safety cushion, leave themselves open to being destroyed by black swan events.

Flashbots

Flashbots were introduced as a solution to the inefficiencies within gas auctions and the gaming of miner extractable value (MEV), which had caused gas fees on Ethereum to soar throughout 2020.

This issue had become so serious by the start of 2021 that some commentators saw it as an existential threat for Ethereum. Flashbots were therefore an extremely important innovation that brought fees down and began the process of returning retail investors – who had moved to cheaper network alternatives – back to Ethereum.

The MEV Problem

Flashbots offer a solution to the critical inefficiencies of "miner extractable value" (MEV). MEV is sometimes referred to as crypto's version of Wall Street front-running, and also a, "systemic risk to consensus-layer security and a realistic threat to Ethereum today."

Specifically, MEV measures the profit a miner can make by the process of including, excluding, or reordering transactions in the network blocks they produce.

% Ethereum blocks with flashbots bundles included

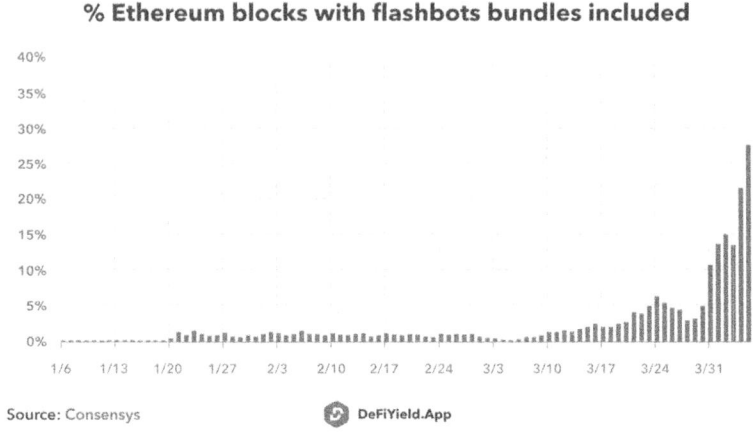

Source: Consensys   DeFiYield.App

That process was previously operated by Priority Gas Auctions (PGAs), which have been described as a kind of "all-pay open auction". Miners naturally prioritize the transactions offering the highest gas price, however the open nature of PGAs made them gameable by arbitrage bots, which constantly bid up gas fees in an attempt to frontrun other pending transactions.

That had the effect of spamming the entire Ethereum network, which in turn, raised gas costs for all network users. That mass frontrunning effort was also responsible for creating key inefficiencies of blockspace usage and network congestion.

According to Flashbots, "MEV risks becoming an insiders' game," whereas they aim to, "Ensure both small and large participants have equal access to low-level financial primitives and that core

Ethereum properties are preserved."

How Flashbots Solve the Front-running Issue

Flashbots introduced a 'sealed-bid' model to replace the open, all-pay auctions. This technique would involve zero gas transactions but would also require a separate fee to be sent directly to miners when a transaction completes.

In this way, Flashbots provide a communication channel between

traders and miners that allow inefficient gas bidding wars to occur off-chain rather than on-chain, thereby reducing network congestion.

As of March 2021, at least 58% of Ethereum network hashrate was reported as accountable to Flashbots. Arguably, this innovation will prove to have more impact on gas fees than the much-anticipated Ethereum EI-1559 updates.

MAIN TAKEAWAYS FROM THIS CHAPTER

Decentralized finance (or DeFi), is an ecosystem of protocols, applications, investors and traders that use smart contracts to perform financial transactions in an open, permissionless and transparent way.

In DeFi, smart contracts facilitate relationships in the same way that banks, payment providers, financial exchanges and other intermediaries have done for centuries in traditional finance.

In order to access DeFi, you will need the internet, a PC or smartphone and a DeFi wallet. Well-known wallets that you may want to consider include MetaMask, Trust Wallet, Trezor and Ledger.

DeFi protocols offer a range of services including lending and borrowing, token exchange, asset management, brokerage, derivatives and much more. Some important protocols to know about are MakerDAO, Compound Finance, Uniswap, Yearn Finance, DEFIYIELD and Synthetix but there are many more. Other important areas of DeFi that you should understand include oracles, decentralized insurance and seigniorage coins.

DeFi projects employ many different business models in order to earn revenue. These include credit monetization, market making, asset management and aggregation of exchange rates. If you want to get started with Yield Farming, you need to understand the main DeFi protocol revenue models.

Decentralized governance, which involves governance tokens being distributed amongst the protocol users rather than being held by a centralized entity or group, is an important benefit of DeFi. Other important concepts to understand include stablecoins, liquidity pool tokens, token standards, flashbots, vampire attacks and black swan events.

IV. THE DEFI INVESTORS RULEBOOK

How do different investors assess DeFi opportunities?

We'll answer that question in the following section, as we explain the definitive rules for DeFi investing. Whether you want to gradually increase your exposure to a new class of assets or boldly seek out the most rewarding yield generation opportunities, this rulebook will cover the core principles of DeFi investing.

First, let's clarify the three main types of DeFi investors.

The Three Types of DeFi Investors

Some investors are only comfortable with a small amount of risk exposure to generate returns. Others are ready to take on a huge amount of risk to potentially increase their returns by an enormous margin. Depending on the risk level taken, all investors can be classified into three main investor types.

The Cautious Investor

The cautious DeFi investor sees an opportunity to generate Yield in a new financial sector with high growth potential. At the same time, they are fully aware of the risks inherent in any emerging market, and they don't want to overexpose themselves.

They generally see the best way of accomplishing their goals is by investing in the most "blue chip" DeFi projects. These are the platforms and protocols which have been around the longest, have the most users, and are the most battle tested. They also believe they must move cautiously, doing as much primary research as they can before they invest in any opportunities.

In general, they will only allocate a minority of their overall digital asset holdings to DeFi. They expect steady, not spectacular, returns as a result.

The Risk-on Investor

The risk-on investor is more excited than the cautious investor about the potential returns that DeFi offers. They're ready to go further, faster, and they want to investigate DeFi's lucrative opportunities for Yield Farming (which we explain later in the book).

In this respect, they are open to a wider range of smaller, less-proven projects than the cautious investor. However, they will still go through a research process for everything they invest in, and they remain wary of the riskiest projects.

In general, they are willing to put at least 50% of their digital asset holdings into DeFi and are highly motivated to generate healthy returns.

The Degen Investor

Degen is short for "degenerate." This investor is totally enamoured of DeFi's potentially huge returns and is willing to risk it all to return life-changing amounts.

They do not restrict their potential investments in any way and are willing to go all-in on even the newest and most unknown protocols. Speed is of the essence for this investor, leaving them little time for upfront research on the team behind a protocol, or the risks that a particular smart contract might pose. All they care about is Annual Percentage Yield, or APY. In DeFi and other traditional investment vehicles, APY is the rate of return, taking the effect of compounding interest into account.

In general, a degen investor is not only willing but feels compelled to dedicate all their digital asset holdings to Yield Farming, even if they risk losing it all.

One important thing to remember about operating in degen mode is that it is only really viable during the bull run part of a cycle, when token prices are rising and are expected to continue in this direction for the foreseeable future. That's because the degen is always looking to maximize yield and this includes the price of a token going up, on top of any extreme gains generated from providing liquidity during the early stages of a token's life.

Which of these three categories best describes you? Knowing what investor type you are at any given time can play an important role in shaping your DeFi strategy.

Approaches for Investing in DeFi

The following table provides a quick overview of the three main types of DeFi investors and approaches they take when assessing various investment indicators.

Investor Behavior   Part 1

Investment indicator	Cautious	Risk-on	Degen
Size and capitalization	Only considers the top 100 protocols by market cap and the top 15 by Total Value Locked.	Only considers the top 300 protocols by market cap and the top 25 by Total Value Locked.	Will consider any protocol with a Total Value Locked that allows them to go all in on it.
Sufficient volumes	Wants to see minimum daily volumes of $1 million, so that large positions of over $100k can be disposed of.	Wants to see average daily trading volumes during the previous 20-30 days of $200k, so a $20k position can be liquidated without slippage.	Does not consider this to be an important indicator.
Platform stability	Will undertake a comprehensive check of the protocol's social media and website.	Will undertake a check of the protocol's social media and website.	Will skim through a protocol's social media and website.
Cyber security record	Will read the auditor's report from back to front.	Will perform a basic search for suspect functions.	Generally is not concerned with this.
Team record	Will perform a comprehensive check of each team members' record.	Will perform a quick check of the key members of the team to see if they've been involved in previous projects.	Doesn't know or recognize any of the team, but does not consider this an issue.
Impermanent loss	Will perform a deep review of the impermanent loss risk and use tools within DefiYield to forecast various scenarios.	Will use their basic understanding of impermanent loss to assess what effect it might have on yield farming returns.	May not understand impermanent loss and is not concerned about it.

 DeFiYield.App

Investor Behavior

Investment indicator	Cautious	Risk-on	Degen
Investment timeline	Likely to remain involved in any single investment for over a year.	Likely to remain involved in any single investment for a few months.	Likely to remain involved in any single investment for a few weeks.
Calculations	Undertakes accurate calculations, such as those to measure the real APY that includes gas fee deductions.	Makes some basic calculations to assess whether the advertised APY makes sense.	Focuses on the advertised APY and rarely considers further calculations.
Budgeting	Will not deposit more than 5% of their net worth in a single platform.	Will not deposit more than 17% of their net worth in a single platform.	Keen to deposit 100% of their net worth in a single platform.
Expected APY	On average, 5-15% return on stablecoins.	15-25%+	Over 150% APY.
Likely investments	Tier 1 lending and borrowing platforms and protocols. For example, Aave or Compound Finance (decentralized) or Blockfi (centralized).	Tier 2 lending, borrowing, exchange and money market protocols and platforms, such as Cream Finance or Venus Finance.	Mostly new and emerging markets, including newly generated tokens and newly created platforms or protocols.
Cost considerations	Transaction costs, including network fees and platform fees, need to be considered. This is particularly true when interacting with the Ethereum network.	Transaction costs, including network fees and platform fees, need to be considered. This is particularly true when interacting with the Ethereum network.	Degens go all in during a bull run, but even then they should only risk what they can painlessly afford to lose. Alternatively, degen "mode" can be used for 5% of a portfolio.

DeFiYield.App

Investment indicator	Cautious	Risk-on	Degen
Risk considerations	Depends on an individual's risk appetite, however it is not recommended to go over 30% of a digital asset portfolio.	Depends on an individual's risk appetite but an entrepreneurial DeFi user may not want to allocate more than 50% of their digital assets to this approach.	Degens go all in during a bull run but even then they should only risk what they can painlessly afford to lose. Alternatively, degen 'mode' can be used for 5% of a portfolio.

DeFiYield.App

DeFi Investment Indicators Explained

You can assess a DeFi investment opportunity in many ways. In this chapter, we will consider the most fundamental methods.

Size and Capitalization

While there is no guarantee that a large project is a safe investment, top projects by market cap and Total Value Locked (TVL) might be considered to be less risky. A DeFi project with $1 billion + TVL has clearly earned a significant amount of trust among market participants. Investors can use this fact to assess the risk involved.

Platform Stability

Passive income products in DeFi usually come with warnings that the rates are unstable, high returns should not be expected over the long term, and funds should not be left unattended. Therefore, it's advisable to research the historical performance of such products, as well as the TVL levels in specific vaults or pools and the reward tokens' performance in the market.

Cyber Security Record

- It is vitally important to assess the safety of locking your funds in a specific product. To be safe, you should assess:

- Existing audits of the platform and its smart contracts

- Any exploits identified, including external attacks or internal project vulnerabilities

- Responses of the project team to such attacks, such as patches or code updates

- Code reviewers' and auditors' background, to assess their reputation

Team Record

Reviewing the background of the team is important because some team members could have previously been involved in scam projects. Such people often use their fraud experience, along with previously stolen funds, to create hype around the new project so they can steal again.

It's also advisable to avoid anonymous projects, which have often deployed their smart contracts with a wallet funded via a mixer like Tornado Cash. Crypto mixers are services that allow token holders to mix their coins with those of other users, which makes it almost impossible to detect the destination addresses to which the coins are sent. This scenario blurs the connections between various wallets' input and output addresses, which makes their funds harder for law enforcement to trace.

Terms of Liquidity Pools

Before adding liquidity to any pool, be sure to understand all major risks involved, especially how impermanent loss can affect your funds. DeFi AMMs are truly innovative in the way they enable anyone to create their own market and define its trading rules. Therefore, if you are providing liquidity for a market, you should review its terms, including the transferability of pooled assets.

Impermanent Loss

If you provide liquidity to a pool with at least one volatile token, it is advisable to research what can happen if its price spikes or collapses. Newly-created liquidity pools and the investors who provide liquidity for them are vulnerable to arbitrage and trading bots. The latter are usually set up to buy a token when a pool is created in order to dump it later.

Later, this book will cover the risk of impermanent loss.

Investment Timeline

Rewards, risk, and time are the three fundamental features of investing. It is even more important to select the right timeline for investment strategies in DeFi than it is in traditional finance because DeFi's immaturity makes it highly volatile and unpredictable.

When choosing an investment timeline, understanding industry-specific developments and cycles is key. With DeFi in a rapid growth and innovation cycle that involves massive inflows of development capability, a project may be considered "well established" even if it has a positive track record of just six months.

Annual Percentage Yield (APY)

In DeFi, the most common way to evaluate investment opportunity returns is by looking at its APY: annual percentage yield. This metric shouldn't be confused with APR (annual percentage return) that reflects the simple interest rate; APY stands for the rate impacted by compounding interest.

To put it simply, when calculating APY, the interest is applied not only to the investment amount, but also to all previously-accumulated interests.

Keep in mind that DeFi projects' declared APYs can be highly volatile, depending on a range of supply and demand conditions within the crypto markets.

Additional Areas of DeFi Investment Research

Once you understand the general principles behind how Yield can be farmed from different projects, it's time to start assessing individual projects to see where the best opportunities exist.

Essentially, this is a process of comparing different projects by weighing their obtainable Yield against their risks. To make these comparisons, you should assess the following features.

Product Value

The most important thing to consider when assessing a project is the nature of its token and whether the token adds value to the project or is merely a speculative asset that isn't really necessary.

Another thing to consider is whether the project's launch has contributed or could contribute to the growth of the DeFi market, or whether it introduces new features that improve the user experience for Yield Farmers.

To assess a product's value, you should therefore consider:

- The problems that the project solves
- What differentiates the project from existing solutions
- The attractiveness of its reward system
- The transaction speeds involved

- The amount of fees paid to the platform
- The availability of voting rights
- The variety of token pairs
- The offered asset-staking ratios

One example of how you might assess product value based on some of these criteria is by comparing a project that utilizes the faster transactions and lower fees available on Binance Smart Chain as compared to the Ethereum blockchain.

Opportunity Cost

Yield farmers always need to be aware of the opportunity cost of either taking or passing on a particular Yield Farming opportunity.

One factor worth considering is how much you have to invest in the first place. For example, if you have $10,000 to invest, you might find that the opportunity cost of implementing a complex or diverse strategy that incorporates many smart contract interactions and levies the related fees simply isn't worthwhile.

The same caution might be wise when you consider utilizing an automated asset manager in order to generate Yield. In this situation, it would make sense to consider the opportunity cost of doing so on the Ethereum blockchain vs an alternative blockchain.

Smart contract security

I discuss smart contract security at length later on in the section "How to Stay Safe While Yield Farming," but it's worth mentioning some key principles that you should understand here.

Firstly, it's crucial that you do not let a project's extraordinary APY distract you from what might be clear security holes or code weaknesses in the smart contract. You must always ensure that no suspicious functions in the code will allow project founders or development teams to exert too much control over user funds or to influence token prices.

Team credibility and public profile

While all projects probably should aspire to decentralized governance where individual founders, developers, or investors don't matter and all you need to trust is the code, the reality is that you must still assess these details within a project's structure.

Building a Yield Farming platform requires a lot of skill and deep technical knowledge, not only of blockchain technology, but also of financial markets. Therefore, you should be looking at whatever evidence is available that demonstrates the project you are weighing up has experience in all these areas.

Moreover, it's important to understand what the project is doing in terms of its marketing, public relations, and communications strategies and whether these strategies suggest the project can be trusted. You should try to see how it behaves in public, what its team has done before, and whether it is sticking to a roadmap, in order to decide whether its actions support its ambitions.

MAIN TAKEAWAYS FROM THIS CHAPTER

There are three main types of DeFi investor: the cautious investor, the risk-on investor and the degen investor.

The cautious DeFi investor sees an opportunity to generate yield but is aware of the risks and doesn't want to overexpose themselves. In general, they invest in the most 'blue chip' DeFi projects after doing as much primary research as possible and only allocate a minority of their overall digital asset holdings to DeFi.

The risk-on investor is ready to go further and faster by investigating DeFi's Yield Farming opportunities. They are willing to put at least 50% of their digital asset holdings into DeFi and to invest in a wider range of less-proven projects but will still go through a research process for everything they invest in.

The Degen investor is willing to risk it all on DeFi's potentially huge returns. They are willing to go all-in at speed, leaving them little time for upfront research. All they care about is Annual Percentage Yield and they feel compelled to dedicate all their digital asset holdings to Yield Farming, even if they risk losing it all.

The main DeFi investment indicators are size and capitalization, platform stability, cyber security record, team record, terms of liquidity pools, impermanent loss, investment timeline and annual percentage yield. Further areas to investigate include product value, opportunity cost, smart contract security, team credibility and public profile.

V. WHAT IS YIELD FARMING?

The phrase "yield farming" comes up often in connection to DeFi. It's key to what makes DeFi so exciting and potentially profitable, but its meaning is not immediately obvious.

Let's begin this important section with a short description of what Yield Farming is. Next we'll work through key topics to sharpen your understanding of this important trend. Our goal is to prepare you for becoming a yield farmer yourself.

Yield Farming is the trading strategy of staking digital assets over a period of time to multiple or DeFi projects and their smart contracts, in order to receive returns (or "Yield") in the form of additional digital assets.

How does Yield Farming fit into DeFi?

Yield farming, which is also sometimes referred to as "liquidity mining," is a growing force within DeFi. It truly took off in 2020, but we can trace its origin back to September 2018 when Compound Finance, a decentralized lending and borrowing protocol on the Ethereum blockchain, released a smart contract that kicked off the whole Yield Farming concept (see more about Compound in the earlier section, "The Most Important DeFi protocols").

Yield farming is made possible by some key DeFi market dynamics. One key factor is that DeFi projects, which operate decentralized applications (or Dapps) made up of various smart contracts, may have several reasons for wanting to hold quantities of a given cryptocurrency in a smart contract. One primary motivation is to provide an exchange market for that cryptocurrency, or to lend it out to borrowers.

However, cryptocurrency holders are unlikely to stake their funds by depositing them in a project's smart contract without being incentivized to do so. This is particularly true for a very new DeFi project, which may not have been audited yet.

Here's where yieldenters the picture.

In return for depositing their funds to smart contracts and having these funds "locked up" there for a set time period

The original token holders are rewarded with additional digital assets.

This is the "yield" they receive.

The "Farming" component refers to finding and capitalizing on various yield opportunities offered by different projects.

Be aware that yield farming is often a high risk/high reward activity! Impermanent loss can increase your exposure to the less valuable token in a DeFi protocol's liquidity pool. As well, there are many scammers trying to entice cryptocurrency holders into depositing their funds, only to steal what's been invested and disappear without a trace. Recognizing these dangers, and staying up to date with the latest yield farming developments, is crucial to investing safely.

Where did Yield Farming come from?

Yield Farming really came onto the crypto community's radar in June 2020, with the introduction of Compound's COMP governance token. However, this momentum had been building since September 2018, when Compound released the protocol that spawned the yield farming industry.

A great deal of innovation had happened in the wider crypto and blockchain industry to enable this important protocol's launch. We will delve into these significant developments later on, but first it's worth understanding more about how Compound's work helped shape DeFi.

The Compound protocol that was released in September 2018 enabled what traditional finance might call a money market fund. Traditional money market funds are a type of mutual fund which invests in near-term instruments that are highly liquid. Similarly with this Compound development, multiple crypto holders would put funds into the protocol, in this case to lend them out or borrow cryptocurrencies.

Depositors would then be rewarded for lending their funds. This reward would come from the interest that borrowers paid the smart contract, in return for the loans that were lent out. This interest that cryptocurrency holders could earn from lending their funds is the first form of "yield" that can be said to have been "farmed."

Yield farming has come a long way from these relatively uncomplicated orgins, of purely earning interest by lending your funds for liquidity provision. And although we've emphasized Compound's role here, it is not the only DeFi protocol that plays a role in yield farming (not by a long shot!). However, Compound's role is very important to understand, because it has been so significant in DeFi's development .Compound is right at the heart of some key milestones.

Apart from the protocol launch in September 2018, another of these milestones came in June 2020, with the aforementioned launch of the COMP governance token (Remember from earlier, that governance tokens give DeFi project users the right to influence strategic decisions about the project's development and how to solve any issues). Governance is an important concept in yield farming, which we will discuss in detail later in the book.

For now, there are two important points to understand about governance.

1. Why a project launches a governance token and distributes it and,

2. What governance tokens mean for the evolution of Yield Farming.

The main reason projects give away governance tokens is to become more decentralized. It allows them to distribute their decision-making power to many different entities. This is so important to Yield Farming because the distribution of governance tokens became a new form of yield to farm.

Why would a farmer want to receive yield in the form of governance tokens? Essentially because they view owning a share of the governance of a project (which is what a governance token represents) as valuable, either now or in the future.

The way a cryptocurrency investor might see value in holding a governance token is similar to how a traditional investor might see value in holding shares in a company. One reason why traditional investors see common stock shares as valuable is because each share comes with voting rights and therefore they represent a share in that company's governance, just as a governance token represents a vote in a DeFi project's governance.

We can expand on this simple analogy by looking at another noteworthy yield farming project, Yearn Finance (which we introduced to you earlier in "The Most Important DeFi Protocols"). Even though Compound introduced a governance token earlier, Yearn Finance took the distribution of its governance token to a whole new level by implementing a "fair launch."

In a fair launch, all tokens are made available to buyers and participants in the project, rather than being held back for founders, team members and privileged investors. The objectives of this approach include full transparency, full decentralization and open governance. Yearn Finance's fair launch had an immediate positive impact on yield farming opportunities, and continues to influence new DeFi projects.

Many of the best-known yield farming projects have gone on to distribute their own governance tokens. They play a crucial role in DeFi, but there are other yield vehicles that are also gaining traction. One example is algorithmic stablecoins, a type of stablecoin

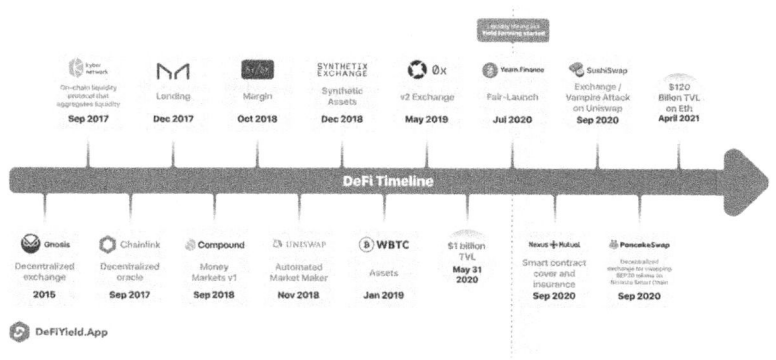

that converge algorithms with smart contracts to calculate price-to-token-supply ratios (see additional details in the earlier section on stablecoins).

If all this already feels like a lot, take a deep breath and don't stress. It's unrealistic—and unnecessary—to try and develop in-depth knowledge of every aspect of DeFi and crypto. That's especially true if you want to launch your yield farming journey as soon as possible.

We understand the urgency. DeFi takes time to master, and there is an undeniable first-mover advantage for early adopters of some protocols. However, jumping in before you know some key DeFi concepts and market dynamics could make you more susceptible to scams. It could also leave you vulnerable to other missteps, as we've experienced firsthand.

Now that you know yield farming's fascinating backstory, let's take a deeper look at how it works.

As with all areas of crypto, DeFi innovation is nonstop. We encourage you to do more research on any topic that you find particularly interesting. Never stop building your knowledge base!.

Types of Yield Farming

Yield Farming is essentially a process of finding the best returns for your assets across several different projects. The returns are the "Yield" and the finding is the "Farming".

There are four main types of Yield Farming, explained in detail below. The common thread is that each type involves locking your assets up for a period of time in a smart contract, so it can use them for whatever it needs before passing your assets back to you.

Why would a project incentivize users to to lock up assets in one of its smart contracts? What will the project do with your assets once it has? We'll explain.

These types of Yield Farming are often interconnected. They recombine endlessly in ways that traditional finance simply can't match. A yield farmer might assess a potential opportunity, and conclude that it can provide yield from:

- lending fees
- liquidity provision
- governance tokens, and
- other types of token distributions.

This can be seen in projects such as Compound on Ethereum and Venus on Binance Smart Chain, These protocols' lending and borrowing may be incentivized by their token distribution.

Yield from Lending

Simple as it sounds, lending and borrowing are key to how yield farmers gain a return on their assets. Throughout history, people have lent money to others in order to generate yield. The yield is the interest rate borrowers pay in return for being given a loan.

It works the same way in DeFi, except the lender and borrower don't have a direct relationship. Instead, DeFi lending protocols such as Compound and Aave show you the interest rates you will be offered for lending or borrowing crypto right on their websites.

If a user wants to participate in the protocol, it's a straightforward path to yield farming with it. ilt's simply a matter of allowing the protocol to interact with your DeFi friendly wallet (like metamask) and agreeing to the terms.

There are some key differences between DeFi lending and traditional lending . DeFi loans are generally heavily collateralized on the borrower's side, meaning the borrower needs to put down a lot of collateral to borrow funds.

This makes the transaction safer for the lender. 'Rates for borrowing and lending are set automatically by smart contracts, balancing requests to borrow assets against assets available to be lent at any one time.

Many would argue that these lending markets are more fair and transparent because they are automated and trustless. They are based almost entirely on smart contract code interactions, rather than the risks of human error or bias inherent in Finance 1.0 and 2.0.

Yield from Providing Liquidity

Earning yield by providing liquidity to a project is more involved than lending and borrowing. However, there are many common threads between the two.

Essentially, projects like Decentralised Exchanges (DEXs) must be able to access sufficient liquidity in a variety of assets. That liquidity enables their users to to trade and exchange these assets. As decentralized projects, they probably wouldn't want to custody these assets themselves. Even if they did, they would be ill-equipped to securely custody the vast quantities of assets required to fund these liquidity pools.

To solve this liquidity issue DeFi borrowed a concept from traditional finance and updated it for the decentralized world: the market maker. A market maker in a traditional finance market does as the name suggests, they literally make a market for a pair of assets by holding enough of these assets, and always being available to trade them when a user wants to. The market maker is a key player in maintaining a market's liquidity.

In DeFi, these market makers become automated market makers (AMMs). AMMs are large pools of asset pairs, orchestrated and adjusted by smart contracts to reflect a mid-market price for those pairs.

This automated price discovery process is primarily driven by arbitrageurs who are:

- identifying a discrepancy between the price offered by a pool and
- the price offered by another exchange, then
- buying or selling the assets in the liquidity pool
- to take advantage of this opportunity.

This is a relatively technical process, however, and needn't be explored in greater depth here to understand yield farming liquidity provision. But now you may be asking, where do these automated pools of liquidity come from?

This is where the individual asset holders, such as yield farmers, come in! Projects incentivize individual investors to deposit and lock up their assets into liquidity pools. These investors are yield farmers who are providing a loan to the platform for the specific purpose of providing liquidity. In return, the depositing/lending yield farmer receives a portion of fees that are paid out to this liquidity pool. These fees are paid by the traders who buy or sell the assets within the liquidity pool.

Yield from Governance Token Distributions

As mentioned previously, governance tokens are one of DeFi's greatest innovations to date.. Governance tokens provide different rights and benefits depending on the project. But they all provide the potential for yield farmers to earn additional returns.

Many projects, in deciding to decentralize their governance, have chosen to distribute governance tokens to their users. In some cases, this means the governance token is airdropped to anyone that has ever used the project for borrowing, trading or whatever services offered. Often, however, governance tokens are sent only to users specifically involved in liquidity provision, or asset lending/ borrowing.

It follows that yield farmers should consider distribution of governance tokens when evaluating the overall yield that a project offers.

Governance tokens can evolve very rapidly, making them difficult to value in terms of their returns. While some governance tokens give holders the right for fees accumulated by the projects, others are less clear about the real returns that will be provided.

In this respect, many should be thought of as speculative. For example, holding the governance token for Uniswap--UNI--does not currently entitle the holders to any fees earned by the platform. However, they do provide voting rights on governance issues and treasury distribution, so it's conceivable that holders could accumulate sizable governance tokens through Yield Farming. They could play a role in voting to add a specific fee-collecting feature to the token, for example.

Yield from Other Token Distributions

There is one more notable type of Yield Farming. That involves the returns you can generate from project tokens that do *not* hold any governance value.

Tokens might be issued for all sorts of reasons that do not relate to governance. These could include enabling transactions within a project ecosystem, representing synthetic value of an off-chain asset, or endless other possibilities. You might decide these tokens hold some intrinsic value, either now or in the future, and decide to farm them to generate yield.

Alternatively, you might not see much intrinsic value in a token at all. You still might decide that its price will rise, however, so you decide to farm this token for selling it at a future date.

All of these potential outcomes should be considered when assessing different yield farming opportunities.

Advantages of Yield Farming

By this point, you're probably sold on the idea of Yield Farming, but let's still recap why this new industry offers such a great opportunity, particularly against the wider macroeconomic backdrop that is overshadowing traditional financial markets.

Yield Farming with DeFi projects provides advantages over traditional investments now, but it also gets you involved in the industry that has plenty of room to grow.

Higher Returns than in Traditional Finance

While APY that you access through Yield Farming depends entirely on the DeFi platforms with which you choose to engage, all opportunities compare extremely favourably to APY available in traditional investments.

As a rule of thumb, token pairs that feature the highest price volatility offer the highest potential returns. The APY range of liquidity pools that are present on the top 10 DeFi platforms can reach up to 900% mainly when we are experiencing a bull run. In comparison, APY offered by traditional investments starts from around 0.1% and rarely goes higher than 5%, even when invested in the riskiest venture capital projects.

When you consider that the average inflation rate is around 2%, most traditional investments are losing value over time. This truth makes Yield Farming a great opportunity for anyone looking to increase the value of their assets in the short, medium, and long term. For up-to-date information on the latest APYs of various Yield Farming projects, check out DeFiYield.App.

Different Risk Levels for Different Risk Appetites

Yield Farming liquidity providers can choose liquidity pools that reflect their risk appetite and profit expectations.

For example, if you are more comfortable with achieving moderate profits that are lower risk, you can deposit money into less-volatile token pairs involving stablecoins, such as USDT, USDC, and DAI.

Of course, you could avoid all Yield Farming and smart contract risk by custodying your crypto with a company like BlockFi, a licensed business under the New York regulator, and gain some limited Yield from doing so. Coinbase Custody or Genesis Trading provide similar solutions for institutional investors, too.

However, this isn't the DeFiYield way. If you're ready to take the highest risks for spectacular returns, your requirements can be met by liquidity pools that contain volatile or heavily-hyped tokens.

Furthermore, investors can maximize their passive income by using automated solutions that rotate funds in search of higher returns. They can also set different strategies that reflect their short-term or long-term goals, rather than be tied into low-Yielding traditional assets with set minimum terms.

No Intermediaries

Yield Farming proceeds in accordance with terms encoded in smart contracts that run on a blockchain, meaning it allows for non-custodial financial activity with no intermediaries involved.

A third party does not need to control acceptance of funds, choose where these funds are invested, conduct transactions, or ensure investment terms are followed. This absence of intermediaries reduces the cost of making investments, meaning returns can be more evenly weighted towards the investor rather than service providers that proliferate traditional financial markets.

In Yield Farming, liquidity providers only pay transaction fees in the form of gas to the blockchain where a project exists.

No Suits

Most ordinary people are completely excluded from interacting with traditional financial markets and the institutions that control them. This world can seem like an impenetrable playground for wealthy bankers in their flashy suits and ivory-tower skyscrapers. DeFi is the complete opposite.

Whereas someone with $1,000 to $10,000 would be given short shrift by asset managers in his bank and told to join the queue of regular customers, that same person is empowered by the gamification and community-driven atmosphere of DeFi to manage the funds on his or her own.

By interacting with DeFi projects and the smart contracts upon which they are based, investors can not only feel independent from intermediaries, but also engage in an enriching experience with like-minded peers rather than aloof and dismissive elites.

Accessibility

For individuals who may have found the range of traditional finance products they can invest in restricted by regulations or a lack of financial institutions where they are based, Yield Farming opens up a unique opportunity to make meaningful returns in freely accessible markets.

The only things these investors need are internet access and funds. Even as a liquidity provider, they can start with any small amount of funds and add to their investments as they become confident from learning more. In this way, Yield Farming is making investing much more accessible for many people around the world.

Diversity of Platforms

The variety of Yield Farming protocols means that investors can select and adjust investment strategies, so they are based on the most up-to-date information about the global financial market or cycles within the cryptocurrency industry.

Although Yield Farming is at an early stage of its development, it already includes an impressively diverse array of DeFi platforms that are all striving to provide innovative reward strategies and optimized user experience. For example, new liquidity pools are constantly being added, with varied token ratios to optimize against impermanent loss and increase risk strategy customization.

Furthermore, we are seeing the spread and diversification of DeFi and Yield Farming onto blockchains other than Ethereum, with Binance Smart Chain being notable examples.

Composability

One of the greatest steps forward that decentralized applications have made in the last couple of years is becoming composable elements of a hugely enriched blockchain ecosystem.

DeFi protocols are often compared to Lego pieces, and a shared settlement layer like Ethereum allows these protocols and applications to interconnect. Therefore, automated asset management projects can make use of decentralized exchange projects or achieve leveraged positions through credit monetization projects.

Two or more pieces can be combined (or 'forked') in many different directions to create a mesmerizing petri dish of financial innovation that reveals something new on an almost daily basis. Anything that has been created before can be used by any entity, and this flexibility allows for an ever-expanding range of possibilities.

Fast Growth

Even though some investors have benefited from Yield Farming already, the industry has plenty of growth potential due to the fact that it provides a great alternative to traditional savings accounts and lending services.

The foundations that have already been laid will serve as a base for further innovation and infrastructure improvements in the coming months and years. These improvements might include:

- The emergence of advanced Yield DeFi platforms, which utilize multi-chain mechanisms and follow higher security standards

- The demand for code security, which would stimulate more auditing agents to enter the market

- More complex investment strategies being invented and spread across the Yield Farming community

- Further development of multi-chain platforms that operate using less gas

- Better communication with project teams, including them giving detailed instructions on smart contract operations and the steps involved in staking funds

Collectively, the work of the close-knit Yield Farming community will result in better security and higher returns for all its members.

Disadvantages of Yield Farming

Nobody said that Yield Farming is easy.

The reality is that big rewards come with big risks, and anyone who ignores the latter part of this balancing act is likely to get burned. The market is constantly being flooded with new projects and new information, the sheer weight of which is almost impossible to track single-handedly. Furthermore, Yield Farmers have to simply accept that they will encounter inefficiencies in what is still a very immature industry.

Understanding the disadvantages of Yield Farming will help you to maximize the benefits you reap.

UX Barrier

Even though one of the great advantages of DeFiYield Farming is that it is open to anyone who wants to take part, the user experience (UX) still has some accessibility issues.

These issues are a problem not only because many DeFi protocols employ poor UX design, but also because users will often need to understand tools like Metamask to get started. In order to solve this problem, DeFiYield has developed a range of tools with simple and easy-to-follow UX that are perfect for new DeFi entrants.

Volatility of Cryptocurrency Markets

One of the most obvious realities that every Yield farmer must accept is that cryptocurrencies remain highly volatile assets, the value of which can change quickly and violently. This fact is significant when your strategy is based around locking your assets in a smart contract for a finite amount of time, as you can be exposed and unable to respond to these changes. For example, if token prices in the trading pairs to which you provided liquidity shift significantly in secondary markets, you might well find that your investments drop dramatically in value.

Complexity of Smart Contracts

As mentioned previously and discussed in depth later, checking and understanding staking terms that are encoded in smart contracts is a crucial part of ensuring investment security. Unfortunately, many Yield farmers don't understand the smart contracts they use and don't bother to find comprehensive reviews or audits about projects they select.

However, DeFiYield is the only platform that audits every single project before listing it. This approach adds an additional layer of security forDeFi users.

Reliance on Gas Prices

Although all Yield Farmers can hopefully look forward to a much more benign gas price environment once Ethereum 2.0 is fully functioning, they still have to deal with high gas prices now and for some months ahead because most Yield Farming projects are using Ethereum 1.0.

Ethereum 1.0 is based on a proof-of-work concept called Ethash that involves miners validating new transaction blocks and being rewarded with fees paid by network users. Miners are of course interested in higher gas prices, so when the network becomes congested, they decide to validate transactions that are paid with the highest gas prices first.

Put simply, liquidity providers have to pay increasingly higher fees just like anyone else using the network, which can make the real returns of any liquidity provision a lot less appealing.

However, the benefit of using Binance Smart Chain or Huobi Chain in the meantime is that you don't need to deduct gas fees from the advertised APY. Also, the DeFiYield cross-chain asset management dashboard provides precise calculations of Farming rewards across chains, which includes gas fees as well as a range of other cost/return metrics.

FUD, Rumors, and Outright Lies

As you start to Yield Farm, you'll notice how many other investors focus much of their attention on the most hyped projects, even if they aren't really bringing a lot of value into the industry.

The community actively promotes and discusses a lot of Yield Farming platforms even though those doing the talking haven't properly analyzed those platforms' economy, token utility, code security, or project development plans.

From my own experience, I can tell you how hard it is to avoid getting wrapped up in a FOMO cycle, but you must remain logical in your analysis and conduct your own comprehensive research.

Scam Projects Abound

The Yield Farming industry is growing extremely fast, and a lot of new projects are entering the market every day. Unfortunately, many of them are scam projects that use the FOMO mentioned to distract investors from doing proper due diligence before they invest their funds.

As a result, we see cases like Unicat, Compounder.finance (not to be confused with Compound.finance, which is a legitimate DeFi project), Groot, SuperMarioBros, and others defrauding investors of millions of dollars-worth of assets. How to identify scams is covered later in the "How to Stay Safe while Yield Farming" section, but you can also always refer to our comprehensive database of scam projects and check whether something is too good to be true.

DeFiYield Safe is the one and only solution that mitigates the risk of scams to keep Yield Farmers safe.

The DeFiYield database of scams, which is the largest of its kind, has been developed to ensure that our users and the wider community can avoid fraud projects. The scam database is available alongside the bug library, automated smart contract checker, and audit database that exist in DeFiYield Safe, a unique machine learning tool that detects and alerts users to approvals of malicious smart contracts.

Hacker Attacks

One of the main reasons that we advocate smart contract audits is because without them, investors are not warned of possible hacker attacks or system errors that can result in rug pulls.

If a protocol stops running properly, the financial information encoded in it gets lost, along with all the funds invested. But even if the dev team finds the code weakness in time and prevents an attack, the project tokens might well still dump because rumors about the risks spread and investors lose trust in the project.

Fraudsters Might Go Unpunished

Cybercrimes are always extremely hard to control due to innovative ways that hackers attack and the absence of a single jurisdictional power that can find and punish them.

Yield Farmers should always be aware of this risk, and proper due diligence will help to ensure they are not caught up in a hacker's schemes. You can also rest assured that DeFiYield is at the forefront of ensuring hackers are not able to get away with their attacks, as demonstrated by our investigation into Compunder.finance that we detail later.

In fact, with our publishing of deep research in this area, we are the only project that is truly busting the scammers.

Yield Farming Risks and Mitigation Strategies

Risks are always evolving and emerging in Yield Farming, so the principle of "research in depth before taking action" must be followed at all times and used to constantly increase your knowledge base.

At DeFiYield, we have built up and continue to improve a foundational awareness of scams and other risky characteristics. This section looks at some of the most common risks we've seen and shows you how to avoid them.

Funds Liquidation Risk

You need to be particularly aware of this risk if tokens you are lending out or with which you are providing liquidity were borrowed using other tokens as collateral. If the price of the collateralized tokens drops by a certain amount, it might mean the leverage threshold has been reached within the borrowing transaction and the collateral is liquidated.

A simple example might be borrowing BTC and collateralizing this loan agreement with ETH. If the price of ETH drops, the value of BTC in relation to ETH increases, which means the borrowed BTC amount becomes increasingly leveraged against the underlying ETH collateral. If the leverage threshold has been breached, the

ETH will be liquidated to cover the value gap.

In most cases, this threshold is 75%, and if it's breached, collateralized funds are liquidated. Therefore, it's crucial to monitor prices of collateralized tokens you use for any transaction.

One way to mitigate this risk is to use advanced price-tracking technology, which allows you to remain informed about potential price changes and react to liquidation threats.

Another approach to controlling liquidation is using stablecoins as collateral. Depending on your appetite for risk and reward, you might also go further and use stablecoins for both the loan and the collateral. An example of this risk minimization approach might be borrowing USDC against DAI. As the value of both assets is pegged to fiat, the likelihood of funds being liquidated because price swings lead to leverage thresholds being breached is very small.

Impermanent Loss Turning Permanent

One of the most significant risks that Yield farmers are exposed to is impermanent loss (IL). It can occur when they provide liquidity to DeFi projects such as decentralized exchanges (DEXes) by locking up funds for a certain amount of time in liquidity pools. If the price of one of the assets in a liquidity pool increases or drops on an external cryptocurrency market, traders will notice an arbitrage opportunity.

Arbitrageurs come to take profit from the price differences occurring between DEXes and other markets. They even out the DEX prices so that they reflect the global market fluctuations.

Let's assume you've provided $10,000 liquidity into a 50:50 pool of ETH and USDT on a decentralized exchange. This ratio means that you've equally split the deposit between these two assets. At

the time of the token staking, ETH was worth $600, so you've pro-
vided 5,000 USDT and 8.33 ETH.

Before The Price Change

5 000 🪙 + 8.33 ◈ × $600 = $10 000

After The Price Change

5 244.2 🪙 + 7.945 ◈ × $660 = $10 488.45

Holding The Funds

5 000 🪙 + 8.33 ◈ × $660 = $10 497.8

 DeFiYield.App

Now, let's consider a situation where the ETH price goes up by
10% on an external market (such as Binance), reaching $660. This
scenario creates an arbitrage opportunity for traders. Having noticed the price difference between the DEX and Binance, the arbitrageurs buy cheap ETH until its price evens out with the price
point on Binance.

The staked funds are adjusted as the AMM rebalances the pool. After the price hike, the total balance amounts to $10,488.45, mean-
ing there are 5,244.2 USDT and 7.94 ETH. This situation equates to
an impermanent loss of $9,35.

In order to mitigate the IL risk, you need to always check how price
fluctuations can influence your Yield Farming results, which is not
easy and can be particularly tricky for a novice Yield Farmer. That's
why we decided to develop an advanced impermanent loss calcu-

lator, which takes into account many factors influencing IL in order to maximize the result accuracy. The calculator is based on a spiral calculation and reflects rebalancing steps that are executed at certain price changes in a liquidity pool.

In order to mitigate the IL risk, you need to always check how price fluctuations can influence your Yield Farming results. This is not easy and can be particularly tricky for a novice Yield farmer. That's why I decided to develop an advanced impermanent loss calculator, which takes into account many factors influencing IL in order to maximize the result accuracy. It is based on a spiral calculation and reflects rebalancing steps that are executed at certain price changes in a liquidity pool.

Rising Gas Fees on Ethereum

Many Yield Farming projects are based on the Ethereum 1.0 blockchain and therefore face scalability issues when the network becomes congested. This congestion can result in a significant increase in gas fees, which are paid when you interact with the network.

The first point to note is that Ethereum is implementing a solution to rising gas fees. Ethereum 2.0 has various updates scheduled that will improve scalability and reduce gas fees. The most important of these changes is moving from the Proof-of-Work consensus mechanism to the Proof-of-Stake mechanism.

As mentioned previously, the transaction fee situation is comparable to the issue of bandwidth on the internet during the mid-90s. In time, the problem will be resolved. For now, though, gas fees are a barrier and a reason why Yield Farmers might consider blockchains other than Ethereum in the short term.

This transition is happening gradually and will result in an even better ecosystem for DeFi and Yield Farming, but you don't need to wait until ETH 2.0 is fully launched to farm Yield with lower gas costs.

One option that is immediately available is to take up the opportunity of Yield Farming on an alternative blockchain, namely Binance Smart Chain (BSC). BSC is more centralized than Ethereum, which can turn Yield farmers away from using it. However, BSC also has benefits, the main ones being low gas costs and higher transaction speed than Ethereum.

Also, users can make big and small transactions on BSC while still only paying a few cents in fees. I expect more Ethereum alternatives to be introduced as the Yield Farming market grows, and these alternatives will likely introduce other options for those looking to avoid rising gas prices.

Flash Loan Attacks

DeFi has enabled flash loans, which are uncollateralized loans that consumers use to finance almost instant arbitrage transactions. However, they are also an important risk of which to be aware.

Because these loans require no collateral to be put at risk, scammers use them to quickly benefit from flaws in smart contracts. These scams take a variety of different forms, but essentially, scammers try to trick smart contracts into acting on the basis of incorrect asset valuations in needed transactions so that they can manipulate prices of related tokens.

To illustrate how these scams work, take a look at some examples from the recent past.

The Top 17 DeFi Hacks Of 2020   Part 1

	Project name	Date	Value of the Loss
1	Lendf.me & dForce	19.04.2020	$25,000,000
2	Harvest Finance	26.10.2020	$24,000,000
3	Pickle Finance	21.11.2020	$19,700,000
4	Eminence	28.09.2020	$15,000,000
5	Compounder	26.11.2020	$11,000,000
6	SharkTron	09.11.2020	$10,000,000
7	bZx (2)	13.09.2020	$8,000,000
8	Maker	12.03.2020	$8,000,000
9	Warp Finance	18.12.2020	$7,700,000
10	Origin Protocol	17.11.2020	$7,000,000
11	Value DeFi	14.11.2020	$6,000,000
12	Cheese Bank	16.11.2020	$3,300,000
13	Akropolis	12.11.2020	$2,000,000

DeFiYield.App

The Top 17 DeFi Hacks Of 2020   Part 2

	Project name	Date	Value of the Loss
14	Percent Finance	04.11.2020	**$1,000,000**
15	bZx	14.02.2020 & 18.02.2020	**$954,000**
16	YAM	22.09.2020	**$750,000**
17	Plouto	30.10.2020	**$700,000**

DeFiYield.App

The dYdX Attacks

The first significant flash loan attack took place on the dYdX protocol. The scheme was based on leveraging five DeFi protocols within one transaction in order to manipulate token prices and bank profits within a few seconds.

The attacker executed the following steps:

- 10,000 ETH were borrowed as a flash loan.

- The loan was split and forwarded to other lending platforms such as Compound and Fulcrum.

- The first tranche of ETH was collateralized in order to borrow wBTC on Compound.

- Another tranche was sent to Fulcrum and used to open five short positions for ETH against WBTC.

- This action led to the Fulcrum smart contract buying WBTC.

- Information about this transaction was then sent to Kyber, another DeFi protocol.

- Kyber then executed the buy order on Uniswap.
- At the time, liquidity on Uniswap was low and the price of WBTC was therefore inflated.
- The inflated price meant that Fulcrum overpaid for the WBTC purchase.
- As the price pumped on Uniswap, the attackers exchanged the WBTC loan taken on Compound to ETH, using Uniswap.
- They then banked the profit and repaid the flash loan on dYdX.

To summarize, the problem was caused by a flaw in the bZx smart contract that Fulcrum used, which was tricked to overestimate the value of WBTC.

The second attack took place in the same week as the first one and also utilized flaws in the bZx protocol. However, this time the scammer was able to trick the smart contract by overestimating sUSD. After the flash loan was paid off, the attacker took the profit and the platform had to deal with under-collateralization.

The Value DeFi Attack

A much bigger flash attack happened on Value DeFi in November 2020.

The platform was exploited for almost $6,000,000, when the scammers used two flash loans to execute the scheme. They first took a flash loan of 80,000 ETH from Aave and borrowed additional 116,000,000 DAI on Uniswap through the flashswap.

They then used these funds to exploit the MultiStables vault on Value DeFi. The scammers executed a series of swaps between USDT, USDC, and DAI to undermine the pricing logic applied by the vault's withdrawal method.

This situation resulted in a dump of the protocol's native token from $2.76 to $1.99.

Code Weaknesses in Smart Contracts

Before I move on to explain the risks that I class as clear scams, let's look at how some projects can, intentionally or not, introduce code weaknesses that may put Yield Farmers' funds at risk.

Even when a project has got a positive reputation throughout the Yield Farming community, code weaknesses can still present a problem of which even the project's dev teams are not aware. In the Wild West that is the emerging DeFi industry, it's often only a matter of time before hackers exploit these security flaws.

These are the sort of flaws that you wouldn't find unless you are experienced with smart contract audits – a topic I will address later. However, protection from scams is one of the unique benefits you receive from using DeFiYield.

As mentioned previously, DeFiYield is the only team that performs audits for free and for the benefit of the community. We believe that the payment auditors receive for their work makes them biased. We don't receive payments because we want to remain independent, so we can fight scammers for the DeFi community's benefit.

In doing so, we are supporting legitimate projects and their founders in building Finance 3.0 for everyone. Many projects do not fit into this category though, and even more smart contract vulnerabilities put users at risk.

Therefore, it's worth telling the story of some projects where our audits resulted in significant improvements.

The Deus Finance Smart Contracts

Deus Finance is a good example of the process DeFiYield goes through in analyzing smart contracts and communicating with project teams to make changes to their smart contracts that will protect the Yield Farming community from danger.

It was also a positive example of a Yield Farming project being responsive and flexible.

When I audited the project, I identified that the staking process was insufficiently decentralized. The staking smart contract owner had a lot of permissions, such as an opportunity to transfer all rewards and staked tokens to any address without any timelock. I therefore rated Deus as a high risk opportunity for Yield farmers, based on the project's development being fully dependent on the smart contract owner's decisions.

In response to my analysis, one of the Deus team claimed that the highlighted code features were required as a temporary platform development step. He then tweeted that the contract ownership had been transferred to a DAO on Aragon in order to decentralize governance. This new ownership model looked much more trustworthy, as crucial smart contract term changes could be implemented only through a voting process. However, 23% of DEA tokens were laid in an EOA, which was still an issue. Again, I shared this fact with the public.

The changes that had been implemented led me to update the project risk level to medium, as a team-initiated token price dump could still occur. Eventually, though, this final 23% of DEA tokens were transferred to the Aragon DAO smart contract. With all the changes and the compromising factors eliminated, I was able to change the smart contract risk level to low.

Deus had made clear steps towards decentralization as a result of the DeFiYield audit, and the affair demonstrated how we can help to keep the community safe.

The Bundles Finance Smart Contracts

Another way that code weaknesses can be identified is through the DeFi community's attentiveness and proactive actions. This was the case with Bundles Finance.

The story began with a warning from a member of the DeFiYield team, indicating that the project's smart contract code contained high risk issues. Specifically, the drain function was revealed, which could be executed allowing the contract owner (an EOA) to drain liquidity pools at any time.

The Bundles Finance team noticed this warning and admitted the code must be corrected. In fact, the project's founder published a video with a detailed explanation of the situation. He explained that the smart contracts had been audited by SolidityFinance prior to the platform being deployed. However, after that, a member of the project's external development team decided to add the drain function as a code security enhancement. The idea was that if something happened to the smart contract functionality, funds would not be locked in it and their withdrawal could be managed.

As the Bundles Finance founder pointed out, the fact that the developer had not communicated the addition of the drain function or the rationale for doing so to the project managers was an internal communications failure.

Eventually, Bundles Finance contacted Solidity with a request for new contracts deployment. As a result, funds staked with the insecure smart contract version were withdrawn to liquidity providers. Staking was paused until a new smart contract code could be deployed and externally audited.

This case was another example of how we help DeFi projects to become more trustworthy, transparent, and safe for the community.

The Alpha Homora Case

Unfortunately, some projects don't react to warnings and recommendations regarding improvements that should be made to their smart contract codes. While it would be wrong to say these projects could be high risk, the opportunity for a token price dump remains, and the community must be warned.

An example of this scenario occurred in my auditing of Alpha Homora, which Alpha Finance Lab developed in December 2020. The process began when I revealed some unacceptable smart contract code details, as follows:

- The project conducted a premine of 1,000,000 ALPHA tokens to a wallet marked as Alpha Deployer.

- The tokens were transferred to another EOA wallet.

- 96% of the total token supply was under the control of the project deployer.

The project team was allowed to mint tokens anytime.

The nature of Alpha Finance Lab posed a risk of centralization, and I informed the community about my findings. After a while, I entered communication with Alpha Finance Lab, and they initially tried to eliminate these concerns in the following way:

They said that all cross-chain platforms couldn't function in a fully decentralized manner. The fact that all user tokens were locked in one Ethereum EOA was absolutely fine, as they could only be unlocked when a requested transfer was performed to the same address on Binance Smart Chain. (This argument referenced some famous projects, saying they had followed the same centralized principles.)

1. They said the infinite minting had been enabled for some potential protocol updates and the developers didn't intend to

apply it.

2. They defended the fact that the project admin fully controls the smart contracts of Alpha Homora by mentioning other projects where the centralized control of smart contracts existed.

3. The team also pointed out that the Alpha Homora team was not anonymous.

It is certainly true that the project team is not anonymous and has a pretty active public facing team. However, the smart contract's code did not back up any of the team's arguments.

Moreover, transactions that can be tracked on Etherscan prove ample reason to doubt the user funds' security Liquidity providers are supposed to just trust the project's intentions, which goes against the important crypto principle of, "Don't trust. Verify."

Even though this project has gained a lot of traction, 98% of the user tokens are still locked in the single EOA under the Gnosis Safe smart contract, and five project owners can perform any transactions with these funds without any timelock. The team can sell all the tokens at any time on any exchange and rug pull all liquidity currently available on the platform. All of this was discussed with Tascha, the founder of Alpha, in the Lobster DAO telegram group.

Therefore, this is a good example of how DeFiYield identifies potential issues in smart contracts so the community can make the best decisions about where to place funds, regardless of how big or well known projects get.

At the same time, please note that DeFiYield does not expect Alpha Finance to perform a rug pull or exit scam because it is backed by Multicoin Capital and Defiance Capital, who are major, high-profile VC firms. You can find out more in our in-depth report on Alpha Lab infinite minting.

Scam Projects

Some projects are scams, plain and simple.

I come across projects that are actively aiming to deceive users almost every week. They take advantage of the fact that high Yield Farming returns make some people less cautious about risks and only interested in rewards. They also take advantage of the avalanche of information about new projects that is generated every day and the difficulty most people have in sifting through it all to separate signals from noise.

Furthermore, most of these scam projects are designed by highly technical individuals who take advantage of the average Yield Farmer's inability to audit smart contracts. However, I cannot emphasize enough how important smart contract audits are for scam identification. Fortunately for you, DeFiYield's experts perform these audits every day to keep the community safe, which is why we are building the largest scam database to keep you from being deceived.

Well explain the methods we use for auditing smart contracts a little later, but let's start with a brief look at some of the scams we have identified to show how they work

The 'One-click Rugpool' Scam

This type of scam has occurred across a number of projects, including the Unicat scam, which involved a rug pull of $200,000.

The Unicat scam wasn't noteworthy for the amount stolen, but because it highlighted a dangerous back door, which allowed the scammers to drain all Ether from users' Metamask wallets. All the users had to do was approve the scam project's smart contract once to expose their funds to the scammers and potentially lose all of them.

The first thing to note about the Unicat scam was how it used a name similar to that of a famous project – Uniswap. It is common for scammers to try to attach their projects in the minds of their victims to some well known brands, even though these legitimate projects have absolutely no connection to scammers.

Victims of Unicat were duped into allocating their UNI tokens into Unicat's fake Yield Farming project in the expectation that they would be rewarded with MEOWs – the native token of Unicat. However, malicious code had been developed that allowed the scammers to withdraw the victims' UNI tokens.

This withdrawal occurred once the victims had approved the Unicat contract. Instead of using these funds for staking, as had been outlined in the rewards incentive, the contract deployer was able to take the deposited tokens without limitations.

The specific back door used involved anyone with ownership of the smart contract being able to call the setGovernance function. This gave them the right to control any transactions, including transferring staked funds to any address:

Here's how the actual code appears:

```
// Set governance contract. Can only be called by the owner or governance
contract.
    function setGovernance(address _governance, bytes memory _setupData) public
onlyOwnerOrGovernance {
        governance = _governance;
        (bool success, bytes memory returndata) = governance.call(_setupData);
        require(success, "setGovernance: failed");
```

Another important point to note about this scam was the fact that the funds stayed under the control of the scammers even after they were withdrawn from Unicat's smart contract. As a result, every user that had ever approved the smart contract had to revoke that approval or risk further fund losses.

It is important, therefore, to always use tools that check token allowance. Many other smart contracts utilize unlimited token approvals, as they claim it improves the user experience because users don't have to validate all future transactions. The problem with this policy is twofold:

- The smart contract has unlimited control to transfer deposited funds wherever it likes.
- The approval doesn't expire, so control over users' funds remains forever.

The final aspect of the Unicat scam that is worth noting is the use of the Tornado cash smart contract, which was applied to remove all traces before the scam. The Tornado cash smart contract allows an EOA to be hidden, thereby allowing scammers to pay ETH to deploy their smart contracts and stay untraceable.

Fortunately for DeFiYield users, one of our newest tools is specifically designed to check for these one-click rugpull back doors and help you ensure you have not approved any.

The YFFS Scam

Another rug pull that the Yield Farming community has had to deal with in recent months was that from YFFS.

This time, users lost around 300 ETH, worth around $130,000 at the time, that had been invested in a pre-sale phase which lasted no more than a minute.

Once again, you can see the pattern of mimicking a well known and well respected project in the way the scam was named. Once again, it's worth reiterating that YFI and YFFS have nothing to do with each other.

When I first audited YFFS, I revealed various issues that made it highly likely to be a scam and DeFined it as very high risk. The fact that the contract owner could pause transactions and transfer staked tokens put user funds at risk. Furthermore, the funds staking contract was owned by an EOA, which could call the stop, start and deposit functions. The first one of these was probably the riskiest, as it allowed the dev team to stop the staking contract and transfer all deposited tokens into their wallet.

I immediately informed the Yield Farming community on my social media accounts. Initially, the team behind YFFS noted my warnings but did not make any improvements to rectify the issues highlighted. In fact, they disputed my assessment. However, I continued to insist that the centralized control over user funds had to be eliminated. Interestingly, I was accused by a lot of community members of spreading FUD.

While these debates were going on, the YFFS team pretended to be cooperative and then agreed to edit the problematic code.

I had suggested renouncing ownership of the token smart contract and adding a timelock to prevent the centralized execution of the aforementioned functions as soon as possible. In response, they decided to burn the admin key and called the transferOwnership and setGovernanceAddress functions, in order to set a 0x000 address as the ownership transfer parameter for the YFFS DeflationStake contract.

These might have been positive steps but they were actually part of the team's deception. Maybe they made these initial changes in order to buy themselves some time as, in the end, they managed to steal user funds.

The Compounder Finance Scam (and How We Will Find the Scammer)

As mentioned previously, the biggest scam to hit the Yield Farming industry so far was the Compounder.finance scam. It is one in which I personally lost $1,200,000, and users lost $12,000,000 overall, and it's an important story to tell for a number of reasons.

Firstly, it shows the sheer scale of possible Yield Farming losses and why you should always be on guard against the risks this industry poses. Secondly, it demonstrates how even experienced yield farmers with smart contract auditing experience can be scammed and why you should always aim to deepen your industry knowledge.

Finally, and most importantly, the story shows that by working together as a community to help make Yield Farming as safe as possible, we will ensure that scammers don't get away with their criminal activity. That's because, as you will see in my explanation of this scam, I will reveal the exclusive information we have that will ensure the scammer will be caught.

HOW DID THE COMPUNDER.FINANCE SCAM WORK?

DefiYield.App
@defiyield_app

Message to the scammer of compounder.finance just scammed approximately $10,800,000

I have personally lost approx. 1m$ and the rest of the crypto community lost approx. 10m$ from your rug pull.

1:16 PM · Dec 1, 2020 · Twitter Web App

The Compounder.finance scam involved the use of a backdoor in the smart contract that allowed the contract owner to drain all user funds. The scheme couldn't be traced on the public blockchain, as a mixer was used to launder the loot.

However, since the incident occurred, we've been investigating and have uncovered the scam's mechanics.

We were able to identify the rug-pull technique Compounder.finance applied, which was based on introducing a special role into the smart contract called Strategist, which belonged to the scam team. A list of exclusive terms were encoded that allowed Strategist to call specific functions for transactions with the platform tokens.

Strategist could call an 'inCaseTokenGetStuck' function followed by a token withdrawal function at any time and without any preventive mechanism for controlling the triggered processes.

```
function inCaseTokensGetStuck(address _token, uint _amount) public {
    require(msg.sender == strategist || msg.sender == governance, "!governance");
    IERC20(_token).safeTransfer(msg.sender, _amount);
}

function inCaseStrategyTokenGetStuck(address _strategy, address _token) public {
    require(msg.sender == strategist || msg.sender == governance, "!governance");
    IStrategy(_strategy).withdraw(_token);
}
```

We have also discovered that Compounder.finance used the Tornado cash smart contract for the same purpose as Unicat did in its scam.

WHAT HAS BEEN THE RESPONSE?

As soon as the scam occurred, the project's website and all related accounts were instantly removed from the web. Therefore, it initially looked like the scammers might have gotten away with an extremely sophisticated plot. However, as you will see, DeFiYield has been at the forefront of tracking them down and we are confident they will be caught.

Our investigation began by looking at the scam transactions that had occurred. We also looked into analysis that others had done, which included reading a report from SolidityFinance that had audited Compounder.finance before the scam but not revealed any backdoors.

DeFiYield also became the coordinator of a victim group of about 600 people from various countries. The investigation was building momentum, and we started a cooperation with a blockchain forensic agency to dig even more profoundly. Now, we have officially filed claims against the scammer(s) in three jurisdictions.

HOW WILL THE SCAMMER(S) BE CAUGHT?

Throughout our investigation, we have been sharing information with the public about how the scam occurred, to ensure that yield farmers are aware of the techniques used and do not fall foul of them again as well as to show the community that the net is tightening on the scammer(s). We can now reveal exclusive information from our cooperation with the blockchain forensic agency, demonstrating how the scammer will be caught.

The key bits of new information are presented in the following graphic and then explained on the next page.

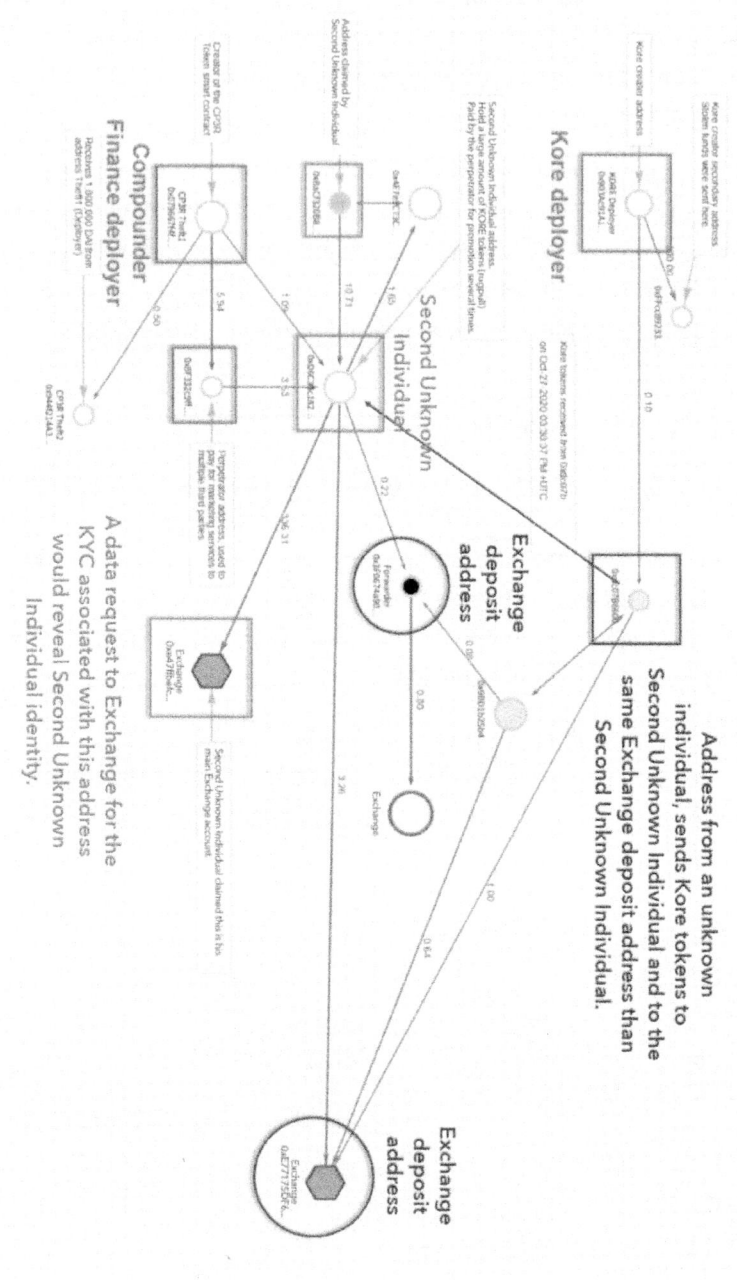

The blockchain forensic agency report that contains this visualization uncovered several leads:

The perpetrator used a well-known international hosting provider, which is likely to have information associated with the perpetrator or an accomplice.

- The perpetrator registered domain names on the registrar Public Domain Registry, which may have the perpetrator's or an accomplice's information.

- Compounder Finance used common social media platforms to communicate with investors, so this social media may have information associated with the perpetrator's account.

- Specific addresses receiving payments from the perpetrator received ETH from a prominent exchange, which may therefore have information regarding those addresses' ownership.

- The perpetrator also used a widely-used hosting provider in Russia, and obtaining the associated data could reveal his/her/their identity.

- An individual helped the perpetrator in several frauds. His identity and details of a potential second individual who could also be involved can be retrieved by contacting the exchange.

Now, the investigation started with these leads. It's only a matter of time before the authorities catch up with the scammer(s), and we will update the community with more information as and when it is available in the coming months. (Names has been omitted)

MAIN TAKEAWAYS FROM THIS CHAPTER

Yield Farming refers to staking funds into different DiFi platforms with the purpose of gaining returns. All Yield Farming opportunities can be classified into four types: liquidity provision, lending, receiving governance token distributions and other token distributions.

The common practice is combining different types and strategies of Yield Farming for yield maximization.

Yield Farming is based on a range of DeFi innovations, such as:

- Automated market makers;

- Automated setting of interest rates and other terms by smart contracts;

- Ability to combine different DeFi opportunities to maximize returns;

- High collateralization of loans, which increases security for lenders;

- Flash loans - uncollateralized loans, where funds are borrowed, used and paid within one transaction.

The main advantages of yield farming include high returns, large variety of investment opportunities for different risk levels and yield expectations, composability, accessibility, absence of intermediaries and fast growth.

Despite the long list of the exciting benefits of Yield Farming, you should always be aware of all its disadvantages and risks: high market volatility, high gas prices when farming on Ethereum-based platforms, FUD and rumors, impermanent loss, UX barrier, complexity of smart contracts, large number of scam projects, high frequency of hacker attacks, flash loan attacks and low probability of fraudsters being chased and punished.

VI. HOW TO SUCCEED AT YIELD FARMING?

——

Now you've got some foundational knowledge about the key concepts underpinning DeFi and Yield Farming, it's time to start getting into the details of how you can actually start generating returns.

In this section, I will explain some general principles that you can use as a basis for all the strategies you employ. These are lessons learned from many months of Yield Farming, not just by me but also the DeFiYield community of experienced Farmers. These principles and the community's advice should start to build your confidence and readiness to get started with Yield Farming.

Then, I'll move on to explain details behind some of the best-known projects in DeFi, which you can start to build into your first Yield Farming strategies. We'll look at mechanisms and incentives within these projects that allow farmers to generate yield. Finally, I'll describe simple steps you need to take to safely start investing.

General Principles for Safe and Profitable Yield Farming

Farming is a game of big rewards and big risks. At DeFiYield, we have learned to try to grasp these rewards while mitigating the risks wherever possible.

In this chapter, I will describe some general principles every Yield Farmer should take to reduce risks and to get the most out of the market.

If you're already investing in traditional finance, some of these principles will sound familiar. Whether you have investment experience or not, some ideas will be new, as they relate to specific idiosyncrasies that are unique to DeFi and Yield Farming.

Get in Early

If a Yield Farming strategy becomes mainstream, you are probably too late. I always focus on the latest market offers and the hottest APY deals, as do other members of the DeFiYield DAO group too, who have all been able to 100x their returns by following this same principle for Yield Farming with various projects.

DeFi projects used to offer early-adopter programs to create a liquidity pillow for an effective start. These programs included higher rates of return and a range of additional financial incentives. I have profited in the past from situations where platforms conducted token distributions among a small number of people.

As an early adopter, you might participate in some projects that go nowhere, but if you don't embrace this approach, you will definitely miss out on the best opportunities. Also, it's good to remember that these wins on early projects can help you build a fund base with which you can make even bigger moves for bigger rewards in a subsequent project.

Don't be Scared by Market Inefficiencies

The crypto and DeFi markets are full of market inefficiencies because they are still relatively immature when compared to bigger and more liquid traditional financial markets.

Don't let this scare you; it's actually a benefit you should exploit-because if you're able to spot inefficiencies as opportunities, you'll be able to farm them and generate massive yields before anyone else.

So, instead of worrying about market inefficiencies, do your research to understand them, and develop a strategy that allows you to benefit from them.

Diversify Your Investments

This is a classic investment rule, and it is relevant for Yield Farming.

Just as you'll spot market inefficiencies all around DeFi markets, you'll also see a range of different risks. Rather than dismissing every opportunity as too risky to jump into, you should tailor your portfolio of Yield Farming investments following the principle of diversification to balance out risks.

For example, if you start to assess DeFi projects that exist on chains other than Ethereum, you could decide that these projects are too risky because the underlying blockchains have not been battle tested to the same degree as Ethereum. Rather than miss out on potentially outstanding APYs, though, it's probably better to take the risk, but keep most of your funds in Ethereum's DeFi ecosystem, in case your worst fears are realized.

Do Your Own Research

As mentioned previously, it's imperative that you always research projects you intend to farm as deeply as you possibly can.

I never skip this step, no matter how hyped an opportunity is. It's crucial to dedicate time to a rounded analysis of the whole project and continually monitor all potential changes. APY benchmarks, smart contract security, the team's credibility, and the project's unique features are areas that you must cover.

Fortunately, you'll be able to access the deep research that our own DeFiYield audits gather and feed into the tools we provide. However, our research isn't a substitute for doing your own, which really must become a habit that you never skip.

Think Independently

One part of the deep research habits you must practice is to never blindly follow what DeFi influencers say or the rumors that constantly swirl around the community.

I've covered crypto communications for a long time now, and it's clear to me that certain influencers have far too much power over how their followers act, even though they are far from being experts themselves.

Therefore, I always take time to check whether a promoted investment opportunity has objectively provable benefits that make it worth taking seriously, and I never blindly follow DeFi market influencers or rumors inside the community.

Farm with a Large Budget

Yield Farming can be attempted with any budget, but it's generally more suited to one or a few thousand dollars. However, this guideline is only true if you want to stick to the Ethereum network, as yield farmers who use Binance Smart Chain and Huobi ECO Chain can do so with smaller budgets.

Two main reasons lie behind this advice. First, Ethereum transaction fees are very high at the moment, which is likely to be the case until eth2.0 is fully rolled out, probably in 2022. Therefore, when you invest a relatively small amount, the gas costs you pay for making Farming-related transactions can easily exceed your projected returns. Every action that involves staking tokens or withdrawing tokens requires submissions on the blockchain, which require network payments in the form of gas.

The transaction fee situation is comparable to the issue of bandwidth on the internet during the mid-nineties. In time, it will be resolved. For now, though, it is a barrier and a reason why yield farmers might consider blockchains other than Ethereum in the short term.

Second, as mentioned previously, I recommend diversifying your investments in order to mitigate risk. This strategy means your budget will be split across various projects and you'll have to pay staking and withdrawal-related gas fees across all of them. As a result, any yield you generate will quickly be swallowed up by fees.

Impermanent loss, slippage, and other Yield Farming risks must also be considered when defining how much to invest in each project.

Avoid High-volatility Times

While you should always try to be 'early' on projects, you can definitely make a case against being too early. What I mean by this is that I never join any project during the first three days after it has launched. It is almost impossible to find an optimal entry price point that early, mainly because of the high price volatility that tokens exhibit in these early days.

Monitor Whale Activity

I frequently monitor wallets of known whales in order to check which pools they farm. This tactic helps me to define optimal entry points for certain projects, as the movement of whale funds provides a signal of the way the market is moving and of projects that have the highest potential. Two on-chain analysis tools that are worth using for whale monitoring are Glassnode and Nansen.

Learning from Experienced Yield Farmers

It's really important to use the experience of others to facilitate getting into the best strategies as soon as possible. Even though the Yield Farming industry has a small minority of scammers, the vast majority of participants are happy to help their peers succeed and stay safe.

This knowledge sharing is exactly why we have set up the public DeFiYield Telegram group, where you can discuss ideas and learn from other farmers. We encourage you to join this popular group, which is the most advanced Yield Farming group available on Telegram. We also run an exclusive DeFiYield DAO group, which is the most advanced Yield Farming group in the industry.

In the next section, I will provide some stories from experienced yield farmers, including myself, who demonstrate why the general principles of safe and effective Yield Farming are important. By sharing my story and those of my closest associates, I aim to demonstrate how strategies we used resulted in us learning the industry and benefiting from Yield Farming so far.

Overview of the DeFiYield Team Strategy

We, the DeFiYield team, employ a mixed strategy of market buying and Yield Farming that is based around diversification. ETH and BTC make up the majority of our assets, but we also have portfolio portions reserved for DeFi index buying and for active Yield Farming.

DeFi index buying involves market-buying blue chip DeFi tokens.

This process is not complex and is focused on buying and holding the most popular and important-for-the-industry projects. We were in touch with some DeFi projects about participating in their pre-sales or partially acquiring them, but a lack of time didn't allow us to close some deals.

In terms of blue chip DeFi, we have a basket of tokens that includes Uniswap, Synthetix, Aave, and Yearn Finance. We bought some of these tokens at their peak during the DeFi Summer of 2020 and therefore were hit by the bear market at the end of 2020. However, we only sell these tokens when the price goes up a lot. For example, we sold about 40% of our positions in February 2021 after seeing them 3x, but we still hold more than 50% of our DeFi blue chip basket because we believe in them as long-term projects.

Yield Farming is more complex. It requires skilled calculation to get it right. The less-complex part of my Yield Farming strategy involves depositing stablecoins in Compound and Aave, the two major lending platforms, to achieve lower APYs that are more secure and lower risk. However, Yield Farming with higher APYs is a short-term strategy and much more complex.

For example, the early auditing of Binance Smart Chain projects that we did allowed us to get in early on projects like Pancake Swap and Beefy. We joined Pancake Swap in December 2020 when the TVL was very low, but it went parabolic later on. This shift allowed me to make 20x on this project, after which I sold 80% of my position. We achieved similar returns on Beefy as well.

More Stories from our Yield Farming Journey So Far

When we began Yield Farming, we preferred to stake funds in stablecoin pools or pools with a 98:2 asset ratio. We took 98% of our coins with a stable value to minimize impermanent loss.

In the first few weeks, we focused on Farming with YFV and YFII, which involved depositing funds into DAI pools. The results were impressive, with an APY that reached up to 2000% at the time as a result of Farming the YFI token through YFII. This opportunity is a great example of why it's important to get in early, as the distribution of tokens to users started off as 10,000 per week, but this number halved with every week that passed.

This strategy paid off for us in such a dramatic fashion because we started Farming YFI when it was worth $800. Having researched the project in some depth, we could see that Yearn Finance was a truly unique idea and that its governance token had real value. Therefore, in addition to our YFI Farming strategy, we also chose to purchase a significant amount of YFI tokens on an exchange, as we expected the token price to increase. This certainly paid off, as the token hit an all time high price of over $43,000 in September 2020.

Soon afterwards, our success was interrupted by a significant loss we absorbed by Farming with ULU finance. We lost several thousand dollars by staking funds in a 95:5 USDC/ULU pool because the price of the ULU token collapsed by 70% in just one day, turning my impermanent loss into a permanent one.

Having also started testing the Balancer 95:5 liquidity pools, we came to the conclusion that they are much riskier than the 98:2 pools we had started out using. Therefore, our next step was to return to this previous strategy by depositing funds into the 98:2 SAFE/DAI pool.

A couple of other projects that are worth noting because we got in with them early are CREAM and Harvest. We liked that these projects presented clear roadmaps, market vision, innovative ideas, and good explanations of their tokens' utility.

After suffering from the compounder.finance hack, which we describe in much more detail in the next section of the book, our next success came from joining Empty Set Dollar (ESD) and Dynamic Set Dollar (DSD) early on. Again, the lesson you can learn from this success is to always be early. You will find many more of these opportunities if you look out for them.

Just as we succeeded with YFI and Spartan (another well-known Yield Farmer) did with SNX, you will be able to find your own stand-out project. In fact, one area that is worth watching is blockchains other than Ethereum, such as Binance Smart Chain, where the next YFI or SNX is likely to occur.

The other point to make about my ESD and DSD successes is that they came from seigniorage coins, which is an area that has been extremely profitable for us and one that we'll explain in more detail later on.

Finally, we should note that getting in early on some defi protocols built on Binance Smart Chain, such as Bifi and Autofarm, was also highly rewarding.

Ask the Community for Help

While DeFI has many untrustworthy entities that are looking to scam you or use some insider knowledge to ensure you get rekt, many, many more people with good intentions can help you. The DeFiYield Telegram channel is a great example of a group where novices can ask questions and source genuine assistance from more experienced Farmers.

It really is important to find a like-minded group of Yield Farmers who can help you stay safe and succeed. This industry gives you so much to think about, and so much can change that it can be really overwhelming to keep up. For all these reasons, you need to be accessing these nuggets of information on an ongoing basis.

That's exactly why we set up the Telegram channels, and as you can see from the following user comment, the community recognizes this value too:

> *"I was hoping to find a serious group of members because I really believe we can help each other a lot. We can win if we are all hard working, vetting projects and having good discussions with substance. I'm looking forward to bringing value to the group."*

What the DeFiYield Community Says about Yield Farming

The DeFiYield Telegram community is a truly unique resource that includes both the main public group for everyone to discuss new and existing projects, as well as the exclusive DAO group for the top level of Yield Farming experts. The DAO group is a collection of Yield Farming OGs that includes the founders of many successful DeFi projects.

As a new or relatively inexperienced Yield Farmer, you can access the main channel and it will become one of your most useful resources for learning about the best projects and strategies. As you develop your knowledge, you might be invited to join the DAO group and discuss these topics with a group of expert peers.

However, rather than wait to be able to access this exclusive knowledge, I want to share the thoughts of some of our experienced DAO members regarding lessons they have learned so far. The comments below come from the DeFiYield Telegram channel and our private group. Some of it tallies with the lessons and general principles I have already outlined, but some will contain completely new insights for you.

"Get in early and make sure to harvest and sell. Don't hang on waiting with your crops too long. They all go bad."

"Don't go chasing every new project. Look at the utility of any project or token over the hype. Look for teams with goals and ones that already have the development to back it up."

"I have learned to not FOMO in before I understood what I was getting into. I'm also starting to do better due diligence, like evaluating front end code for errors in APY calculations."

"I generally avoid high Yield farms these days. Seigniorage is an exception because I know I can play it well. Otherwise, I pick projects that I like and, if they Yield 100%+ APY, then it's a bonus."

"Decisions based on extreme fear or euphoria are both likely to get you rekt very quickly. It's tough to be rational during FOMO fever, especially as there have been some cases where it really hurts to miss out, but one mistake is enough to be totally rekt. It's better be careful and suck it up if the lost opportunity moons later."

"My biggest mistake was probably overselling mining rewards during dips. Sometimes it's better to hold clearly oversold coins. However, it's hard to know whether something will death spiral vs whether it will recover."

"In a bull run don't take 100% of profits, leave some for the home run. In a bear market, no low is too low, so it's best to cut your losses."

"Keep records so you can learn from your successes and mistakes."

"[A paid] audit means nothing. They don't test for outside attack vectors. DeFiYield technical review is way more comprehensive. Risk doesn't go away just because it got audited."

"If you wanna Yield farm, don't become the Yield."

Use Full Suite of DeFiYield Tools

Apart from our community, you can use many tools to avoid scams and get a fuller picture of any projects in which you are interested. For example, we are making the biggest database of scams to avoid and also alerting you to scam projects that are linked to your MetaMask.

Auditing Smart Contracts

Auditing smart contracts is an absolutely crucial part of staying safe while Yield Farming.

However, remember that a project-paid audit is only valid at the point when it is published because the project's developers could make changes to the code. You need to ensure you are tracking changes and always remember that Yield Farming is risky. Invest only part of the capital you have available and always do your own research.

DeFiYield's Safety Commitment to Smart Contract Audits

1. We are not paid for audits. We perform an agnostic technical review for the benefit of the DeFi community.

2. We only audit projects that the DeFiYield community wants. You can submit a request for an audit, and if this request is upvoted by the community, we will audit the project.

3. DeFiYield is the market leader in free and independent audits. We are the only team with the unique ability to perform free audits for the community's benefit.

4. DeFiYield's free auditing helps the DeFi community to fight

scammers. We support legitimate projects and their founders in building Finance 3.0 for everyone.

5. We will continue to pursue scammers until the last one has been defeated.

6. The search for scammers and the ongoing need to protect the DeFi community motivated us to write The Wall Street Era is Over and offer DeFiYield Safe.

Our Approach to Auditing

At DeFiYield, we always interrogate the security of a project's smart contract code and the specific investment terms involved. Over the past four months, we have independently audited more than 40 Yield Farming projects, and we continue to publish more on an ongoing basis. Our work has resulted in the identification of scam projects before they could dupe investors as well as the introduction of security improvements in several projects.

Our audits are a contribution to the community, with the aim of holding scam projects to account and keeping Yield Farmers safe.

Some sites, like Coingecko and CMC, display Yield Farming opportunities, but they do not scrutinize the projects with the same attention to due diligence and auditing as DeFiYield, as their main focus is listing tokens.

In contrast, our work results in tangible security changes, such as the introduction of timelocks. In fact, we can point out 8-10 projects in which our audits have led to specific security upgrades. We are also confident that the work we do in highlighting security issues is leading to many more early-stage DeFi projects implementing better security from the start.

In this chapter, I will break down the main areas that need to be investigated in a smart contract and the order in which it makes sense to do so. Essentially, though, the audits assess five key areas:

- Features of a smart contract system
- Token distribution
- Token location(s)
- Access to staked funds

We also look at security issues that do not specifically relate to the smart contract but do relate to the project's external positioning and its reputation within the DeFi community.

UNDERSTANDING OWNERSHIP

Before anything else, I check a project's ownership structure, as the level of decentralization is an important feature that needs attention.

Ownership is important because it usually plays a role in the functions that a smart contract can call. Certain functions can directly affect the funds that users have staked, the tokens that can be minted, and the distribution of both.

Many projects use external data sources and a special admin key to manage their system, conduct smart contract upgrades, and perform energy shutdowns. While these features aren't necessarily an issue, users should be aware of them, as they involve trusting the project owners to do the right thing.

If an Externally Owned Account (EOA) owns a contract belonging to the project owner and its team, they have the opportunity to call functions in order to conduct an unfair token distribution, which could result in either a token price dump or a steadily worsening project value.

Alpha Homora is an example of what happens when this EOA contract ownership occurs. Alpha Finance Labs controls 96% of the token supply in an EOA wallet. Therefore, they manage the admin keys without any governance in place.

However, centralized contracts can be even riskier if they give project owners the right to access users' locked funds. The owners could transfer funds into their own accounts and exchange them for other assets on secondary markets without any restrictions. In this way, they would suck all liquidity from the project and thereby perform a rug pull.

AUDITING SPECIFIC FUNCTIONS

Each smart contract has its own set of functions and a unique way in which they are controlled. Understanding these interactions is crucial for understanding a smart contract's security risk.

A function should only be considered suspicious when it's applied in combination with terms and parameters endangering user funds, such as centralized ownership and ability to set specific addresses as transaction beneficiaries. Therefore, it's important to remember that a function's security depends on the context in which it operates.

The following section should give you a good idea of the main functions I check, the order that I work through these checks, and the way I assess whether certain smart contract features pose a security risk.

The Mint Function

I always check whether the mint function or another function created for token generation is available, who can call it, and who is the owner of the contract where it can be called. If no hard cap is specified for a token and minting can be called at any time without any restrictions, infinite token generation is a risk. This term means that tokens could be issued in unlimited amounts, which causes their inflation.

Another risk associated with minting can occur if the dev team can call the function at any time and a dev-controlled EOA can be set as the receiver of the minted tokens. This is a very popular rug pull scheme in DeFi that is easy to perform.

For example, the owner of the project token smart contract might mint a million tokens to his wallet address and then sell them out on a DEX for stablecoins, ETH, or other crypto assets with real value, sucking all liquidity out of the trading pairs used and killing the token price. Investors are then left with the project tokens that don't have any value and can't be exchanged for real assets.

Alpha Homora is a project example (which has reached $1.2 billion in total value locked) containing the smart contract flaw mentioned. Following our audit of December 2020, we consider the project high risk.

The Pause Function

The pause function can be risky because when it is called, users don't have access to their staked funds.

If a contract vulnerability is revealed and users need to transfer funds to a safer place, they won't be able to relocate the endangered funds. Scam projects introduce the pause contract function layered with other conditions in order to transfer funds to their own wallets. In fact, this trick was used by YFFS, a scam we mentioned earlier.

At first, the YFFS smart contracts looked safe. However, a loophole they introduced was hidden under the pause function. An EOA belonging to the project's developers owned the staking contract, which could invoke the stop function. Therefore, they could stop the staking and transfer all staked tokens to their EOA wallet, which they eventually did.

The Migrate function

Smart contract migration functionality can be used for a variety of purposes and is not dangerous in itself. As with other functions, the risk it poses depends on encoded conditions with which it is combined.

To understand how this function works, you need to understand that smart contracts remain on a public blockchain forever and their code cannot be changed. On the one hand, this consistency guarantees that embedded logic for execution of transaction conditions will remain the same. On the other hand, this situation introduces issues for developers if they need to make functional improvements or security updates.

In order to mitigate the inconvenience of this limitation, developers attempt to make it possible to make changes to smart contracts. One of the ways they achieve this end is by introducing the migration function.

One of the most common and legitimate use cases for the migration function is replacing an old token with a new one, where the latter will be managed according to the rules that have been coded into the project's smart contract system. In this case, availability of the opportunity to make migrations doesn't bring any risks to users.

However, if smart contract developers retain the opportunity to make changes to the code, there is a risk they will use it to scam users. For example, if developers introduce the migration function into a staking contract, they can add new functionality to the code such as transferring staked tokens to any EOA they want at any time and without the permission of users.

Proxy Patterns

Because an already-deployed smart contract's code can't be upgraded, some projects choose proxy contract patterns. A proxy contract stores variables. Receiving message calls, it redirects them to a contract containing the logic. This architecture allows projects to bind newly-deployed contracts with new logic to already-existing dependencies as if the main logic gets upgraded, which exposes users to the risk of losing funds, as malicious logic can be introduced with a newly-deployed contract anytime

The TransferOwnership function

I always pay attention to whether the possibility of transferring smart contract ownership exists using the transferOwnership function alongside certain parameters.

If this possibility is present, I check limitations on what addresses can be set as new smart contract owners. I also check the availability of some preventive mechanisms for transferring ownership, such as timelocks or approving decisions, to execute these types of transactions through governance voting.

If ownership of a staking or a token smart contract can be transferred to any EOA at any time, and the new owner is eligible to control all funds controlled by the vulnerable contract, this situation should be considered a red flag that makes the project high risk for Yield Farmers.

I immediately warn users about this danger and suggest that developers renounce the ownership in public. If they insist on the presence of the transferOwnership function or ignore my warnings, their actions only confirm my suspicions because even if no direct danger can be detected, the functionality can be used in a cross-function reentrancy attack, which involves combining the vulnerable function with one that an attacker controls..

TIMELOCKS

Projects often introduce timelocks for execution of certain functions in order to convince liquidity providers and other users that the functions are safe. However, this practice never gives a full guarantee for user safety, and I'll explain why. First, though, let's look at what a timelock is in more detail.

The timelock contact or timelock conditions added to certain functions are used to delay a certain process or transaction being performed on a blockchain. Contract deployers utilize them for a few reasons; one of the main purposes is to control token sales on the open market.

For example, a project might want to allow its developers to hold a big share of tokens granted to them as a reward. It might also want to allow investors to purchase a large amount of tokens at an advantageous price at the start of a project's life.

If the project owners want to limit how and when these tokens are sold on the open market in order to avoid a price dump, they can introduce a timelock that does exactly that. This tactic allows them to adjust token holders' incentives to be in line with the project's roadmap and strategy.

A timelock might also be applied in order to reassure users, which can be effective if the timelock lasts long enough for users to notice, understand it, and properly react to smart contract changes and transactions that affect their funds. However, in my experience, timelocks usually don't exceed 24 hours, and this is not enough time to consider them a good safety valve.

Furthermore, when a timelock is the only safety measure imposed on suspicious functions, yield farmers should use special Telegram bots to track the changes and perform necessary procedures to secure their funds in time. Moreover, it's important to understand that some timelock conditions can be bypassed.

Scammers often find ways of moving funds before timelocks expire, even when the timelock contract or timelock conditions have no code vulnerabilities and prevent funds from being transferred for a given period. This trick usually involves transferring future ownership of the locked funds instead of getting a direct permission to move the tokens.

The bypassing mechanism is different for each type of timelock contract and timelocks can be bypassed in many different ways. For most readers, all you need to understand is that timelocks are definitely not a one-size-fits-all solution for improving smart contract security.

How DeFiYield Keeps You Safe

As you can tell from the in-depth details provided in this chapter, DeFiYield does a lot to keep Yield Farmers safe because we want to make Yield Farming a secure opportunity for everyone and to provide the safest route for anyone entering the DeFi ecosystem.

The DeFiYield Safe solution was designed for exactly this user need. It is a machine learning tool that automatically detects and alerts users to instances where they have approved token allowances for malicious smart contracts. This detection is possible because DeFiYield Safe incorporates a range of tools, including the open source Yield Farming scam database, bug library, automated smart contract check, and audit database.

In addition to our unique products, here's a brief summary of the steps we take to keep DeFi users safe.

Auditing Smart Contracts So You Don't Have To

Some yield farmers have the technical knowledge to audit smart contracts themselves. If you're one of them, we encourage you to use your skills and share what you find with the community.

However, for those who do not have the necessary skills, DeFi-Yield constantly audits any project's smart contract that looks like it might provide exceptional yield. We've audited 36 projects in three months, and we share all our findings to help keep you safe.

Furthermore, the DeFiYield smart notification system provides an automated warning system for users that significantly reduces the risk of being scammed.

Notifying the Community When We Find Issues

The reason we audit projects without taking payment for it is to keep the community safe. We provide this service as a gift to the community so we can always remain independent and unbiased. In this way, ours is a totally different approach to auditors who receive around $50,000 per audit from project teams.

When we do find an issue in a smart contract, we immediately notify the community and provide as much information as possible as quickly as possible. This promptness is important because it ensures Yield Farmers can act if any of their funds are at risk.

Additionally, we believe in transparency. We want the community to know what we have learned so everyone can stay safe. This strategy also means users can see our conclusions and discuss them in the open.

Crucially, we have also developed the DeFiYield Safe tool to automatically scan any DeFi project so that users are informed about dangers and can stay away from them.

Helping Responsible Projects Fix Code Weaknesses

As we discussed in the chapter on auditing smart contracts, the existence of a suspicious function in a project's smart contract does not necessarily mean that the project is a scam. All code issues and vulnerabilities found must be considered in relation to other circumstances in order to make a proper project risk assessment.

Therefore, we're also transparent about changes we suggest projects should make to reduce the risks we identify. We understand that some projects may miss code weaknesses or have explanations for them, so we give them the chance to make changes.

Recording Scams in the Biggest Database of its Kind

When we know that a project is a scam, we make sure everyone in the community knows about it. To aid awareness, we are building the biggest database of scams that has ever been assembled and making it available for everyone to see.

And we don't leave it at that. As the example of Compounder.finance demonstrates, we are willing and able to pursue scammers on the community's behalf, filing claims around the world and using our blockchain forensic partnerships to investigate them.

Providing a Suite of Tools to Keep You Safe

DeFiYield is the safest way for anyone to access Yield Farming opportunities that DeFi offers for all the reasons mentioned above. We are also building new tools every day to keep you safe and help you make the most of every opportunity.

We include a tool that monitors your Metamask account and ensures it's not exposed to liquidity drains from projects you previously permitted. We're also in the process of developing a tool to monitor timelocks, which are introduced to functions influencing user-fund security.

Building a Community of Reliable Yield Farmers

The final way we help you stay safe is by giving you access to a ready-made community of reliable and responsible Yield Farmers via our popular Telegram channel. This is not a place full of rockets and moons. In fact, anyone with that agenda is quickly excluded.

Instead, the space is available for experienced Farmers to share ideas, question new projects, and generally help one another with Yield Farming. For those who are new to the industry, it's a great place to watch and learn from others who've been Farming for a while.

MAIN TAKEAWAYS FROM THIS CHAPTER

In order to succeed at Yield Farming and ensure your funds are safe, you should follow classic investment principles as well as considering DeFi's unique circumstances.

You should perform deep research before investing funds in any project. Besides APY evaluations, you should also analyze a project's security, team and the value of its products and services. You should try to get in early before a project becomes mainstream. However, the volatility of the first 1-3 days after a project's launch should be avoided.

Select your scale of investment based on farming costs. As transaction costs are currently high on Ethereum, make sure they don't take a significant percentage of your returns. You should invest at least a few thousand dollars if you want to see notable results. Alternatively, stick to DeFi projects based on BSC or HECO.

Be flexible when it comes to assessing market inefficiencies by using them to your advantage rather than being scared of them. Think independently rather than blindly following rumors or market influencers' opinions but do watch what whales do. Finally, diversify your investments, ask the community for help and learn from experienced farmers.

When you are skilled enough to check DeFi projects' smart contract code, pay attention to smart contract ownership in order to determine how decentralized the project is and what privileges the dev team has. You should also assess the project's governance system, the availability of token minting and the terms of token minting, migration, proxy patterns and timelocks.

VII. THE FUTURE OF DEFI

So far, we have looked at the key components of Yield Farming, including the main dynamics that affect the market, the most important DeFi projects you need to know, and the steps you must take to stay safe.

In this final section of the book, we will look at what the future holds for Yield Farming. What we see now is Yield Farming in its early development phase; therefore, a lot can and will change. It is likely that Yield Farming will grow as a result of many small subsectors blossoming into more substantial sectors in their own right. These sectors will cover new, innovative financial services and technically sophisticated solutions for higher returns.

Therefore, you need to be aware of some of the most important emerging trends, so you can be ready to take advantage as early as possible.

Governance-enabled Growth

Unique governance systems that are developed within the most innovative projects will undoubtedly drive the growth in DeFi Yield Farming. These systems are designed so that users can participate in DeFi platforms' decision-making processes through voting rights. In this way, users are empowered to define improvements that are aligned to their needs and requirements. Some areas of improvement where we expect to see further development in the short and medium term are ones like transaction cost optimization, Yield Farming reward enhancements, and measures related to staked funds' security.

A great example of where this developing trend for user-enabled governance can already be seen is the way users made update proposals for Uniswap's reward system before its expiration. They wanted to restart the Yield Farming program with more attractive rules, as the old incentives had become weak in comparison to those that newly-launched projects offered. As a result, the project's team reacted by updating its smart contracts in accordance with the user requirements.

Avoiding Whale Manipulation

Another reason why increasingly more market participants may be driven towards Yield Farming in DeFi is to counter the price instability of cryptocurrencies on the open markets. Earning through cryptocurrency trading is becoming more risky and complicated by the day for smaller players, mainly because the largest players (often referred to as whales) can manipulate market prices due to their massive trading power.

Their typical manipulation strategy consists of placing large sell orders for selected crypto assets, which causes the price to spiral downward. After finishing the price attack, whales then place a large number of buy orders to scoop up the assets at the lowered price.

DeFi offers a variety of profit opportunities for market participants even when the whole cryptocurrency market is down, which is likely to lead more people into Yield Farming.

Cross-chain Solutions

As the popularity of DeFi increases, projects are becoming increasingly aware of the need to flex their protocols in order to optimize gas costs and transaction speeds for users, which is leading traders to demand the ability to perform transactions across multiple blockchains.

Yield Farmers need DeFi projects to increase the complexity of their architectures so assets can be managed across multiple platforms with different technical features. All of these goals can be achieved by implementing cross-chain mechanisms.

Cross-chain solutions have emerged to tackle the issue of interoperability and thereby increase DeFi adoption, which has already transformed the technological landscape of the industry so that two or more blockchains can interact and exchange value. This value exchange mechanism is called the atomic swap and it will be an area that continues to grow.

An example of a cross-chain bridge with decent liquidity is Anyswap.Exchange, built by the Fusion Blockchain team.

Atomic swaps are based on a set of Hashed TimeLock Contracts (HTLC). No actual computation occurs between the blockchains used, with the two parties involved in a transaction confirming the movement of funds. If one of the parties does not submit within a limited timeframe, the transaction fails. In this way, HTLCs are used as a temporary escrow for the assets and the transaction is only completed when both parties confirm the swap. Decred is working on atomic swaps for Bitcoin.

Aside from atomic swaps, DeFi projects are constantly innovating in order to combine different blockchains' advantages and diversify yield opportunities by using the strengths of several protocols at once. Therefore, blockchain interoperability and cross-chain solutions are key areas to watch, as they will be major drivers behind DeFi's rise above traditional finance.

For this reason, DeFiYield already allows users to manage assets cross-chain.

Binance Smart Chain

Binance Smart Chain Ecosystem　　　　Part 1

Algorithmic Stablecoins

- DITTO MONEY
- BDOLLAR PROTOCOL
- MONSTERSLAYER FINANCE
- IRON.FINANCE
- MIDAS DOLLAR

Entertainment

- BOUNCE
- DEGO
- JUGGERNAUT

Aggregators

- BSCEX
- OPENOCEAN
- 1INCH

Crosschain token swap/ bridge

- ANYSWAP
- BINANCE BRIDGE
- JELLYSWAP
- NERVENETWORK
- REN PROTOCOL

Wallets

- BINANCE CHAIN WALLET
- MATH WALLET
- MYETHERWALLET
- ONTO WALLET
- SAFEPAL WALLET
- TRUST WALLET
- TOKENPOCKET
- COIN98 WALLET
- DFOX WALLET
- BITKEEP WALLET
- MIDAS WALLET

Lending & Borrowing

- CREAM.FINANCE
- FORTUBE
- VENUS
- ALPHA FINANCE

Insurance

- CERTIK
- HELMET
- SOTERIA

Derivative

- HEDGET
- METTALEX
- INJECTIVE PROTOCOL

Binance Smart Chain Ecosystem   Part 2

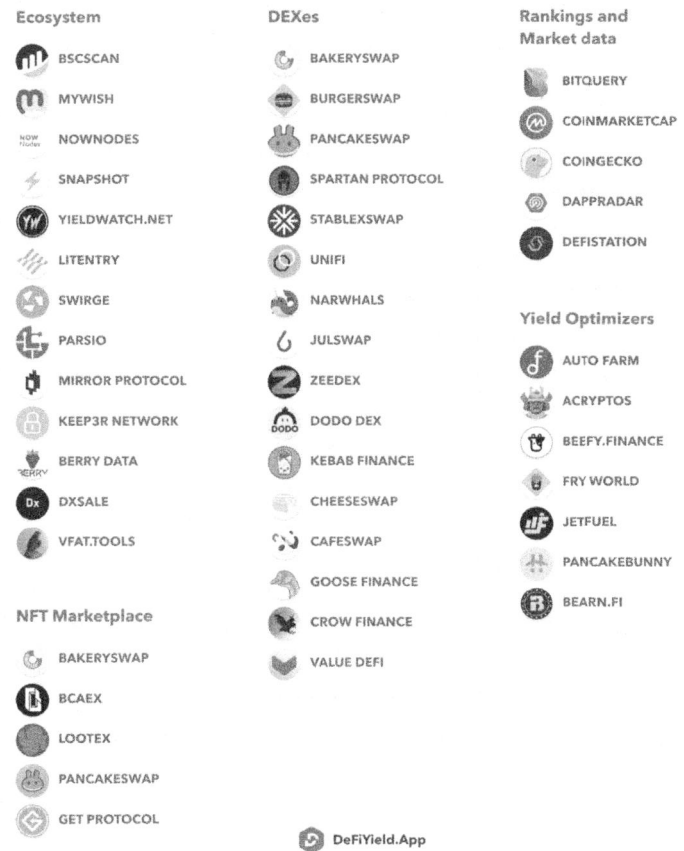

Ecosystem

- BSCSCAN
- MYWISH
- NOWNODES
- SNAPSHOT
- YIELDWATCH.NET
- LITENTRY
- SWIRGE
- PARSIQ
- MIRROR PROTOCOL
- KEEP3R NETWORK
- BERRY DATA
- DXSALE
- VFAT.TOOLS

NFT Marketplace

- BAKERYSWAP
- BCAEX
- LOOTEX
- PANCAKESWAP
- GET PROTOCOL

DEXes

- BAKERYSWAP
- BURGERSWAP
- PANCAKESWAP
- SPARTAN PROTOCOL
- STABLEXSWAP
- UNIFI
- NARWHALS
- JULSWAP
- ZEEDEX
- DODO DEX
- KEBAB FINANCE
- CHEESESWAP
- CAFESWAP
- GOOSE FINANCE
- CROW FINANCE
- VALUE DEFI

DeFiYield.App

Rankings and Market data

- BITQUERY
- COINMARKETCAP
- COINGECKO
- DAPPRADAR
- DEFISTATION

Yield Optimizers

- AUTO FARM
- ACRYPTOS
- BEEFY.FINANCE
- FRY WORLD
- JETFUEL
- PANCAKEBUNNY
- BEARN.FI

At the end of August 2020, Binance introduced its Binance Smart Chain to facilitate smart contracts and become the main alternative for Ethererum in the DeFi space.

By the end of February 2021, the total value locked in projects built on Binance Smart Chain had grown to $9 billion, with Pancake Swap and Venus becoming two of the top projects.

While Binance Chain, launched in April 2019, did not support smart contract interactions and was designed to facilitate trading, BSC was developed to run smart contracts and enable compatibility with the Ethereum Virtual Machine.

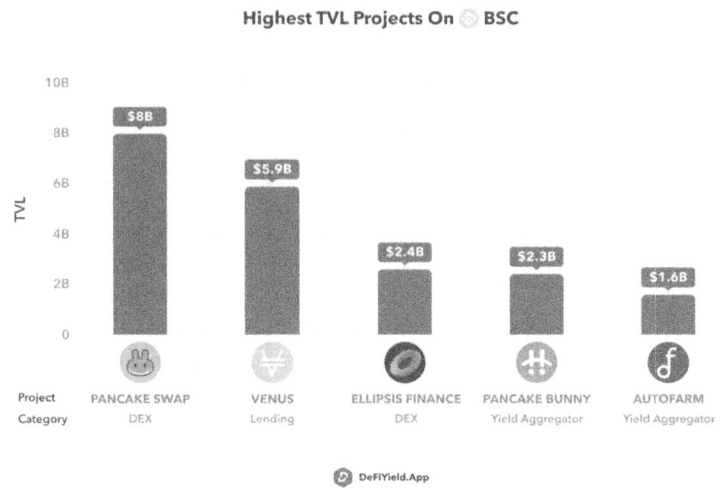

Highest TVL Projects On BSC

DeFiYield.App

With the deployment of BSC, a new token standard was introduced called BEP-20. Developers can use this standard as a flexible format for issuing different tokens with different goals (such as the creation of peg versions of other blockchains' tokens) in order to make them applicable to BSC. Fees for all transactions with BEP-20 tokens are paid in BNB.

BSC can be defined as an extension to Binance Chain, but it is not an off-chain scalability solution for Binance Chain. It functions independently, and smart contracts can be run on it even if Binance Chain is disabled. By developing BSC, Binance's main aim was to enable DeFi projects to relocate from Ethereum, which is why it also made sure that the network is compatible with popular user applications like Metamask. It's very easy to configure the wallet to work with BSC and only requires a couple of setting changes.

A number of effective DeFi apps are already built on BSC, with PancakeSwap standing out as a great Yield Farming opportunity. Projects with similar offers are Autofarm and BakerySwap. Spartan Protocol is another BSC-based project, which was developed as an efficient platform for decentralized derivatives. It includes exchange services and money market offers that are similar to the ETH-based Aave project.

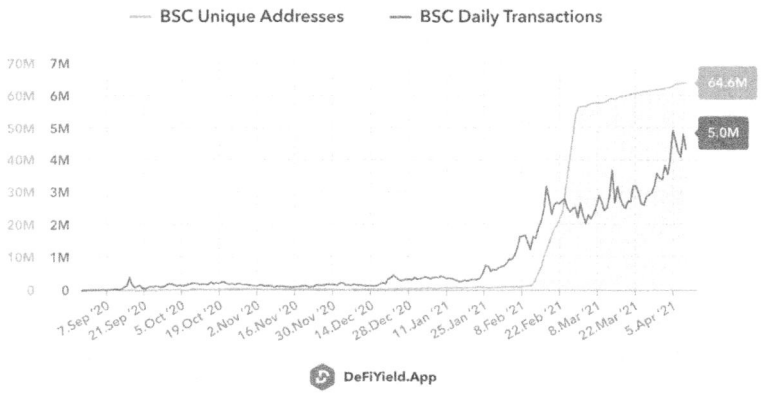

BSC adoption growth

DeFiYield.App

This dual-chain system is important for users, as it allows them to smoothly transfer assets used in DeFi from one chain to another and is why the DeFiYield cross-chain app is also available for Binance Chain and Huobi ECO Chain.

The flexibility of Binance Smart Chain is already having a major effect on the growth of the entire DeFi space. This growth can be seen in the continuing adoption of Binance Smart Chain, with the increasing number of daily transactions on BSC demonstrating how the network is constantly gaining new users.

Huobi ECO Chain

Another smart contract chain that is proving to be a good alternative for Yield Farmers who are put off by the high transaction fees experienced on Ethereum is Huobi ECO Chain.

Huobi is an established cryptocurrency exchange with high transaction volumes and a large user base across the US, South Korea, and other major cryptocurrency locations. Like Binance Smart Chain, it has replicated the functionality of Ethereum in order to drain liquidity from it in what can be referred to as a vampire attack.

Huobi has a lot of customers across the globe and therefore may well succeed at draining liquidity from Ethereum because it can market to an established user base. Just as with Binance Smart Chain, Huobi likely has a good short-term advantage over Ethereum in 2021, at least until Ethereum transaction fees come down when new scalability solutions are introduced.

Interoperability

One of the most interesting developments of the bull run that occurred from late 2020 into 2021 has been the way interoperability between blockchain has emerged. This topic has been on the radar of most people working in crypto for some time, but only recently has it become an important reality for improving the DeFi experience.

Assets can switch between blockchains and therefore enable interoperability in three ways: atomic swaps, bridges, and protocol interoperability.

The most well-known interoperability protocols are Polkadot and Cosmos. Ethereum's former CTO and co-founder, Gavin Wood, created Polkadot, which styles itself as a platform for Web3. Cosmos, which calls itself the internet of blockchains, was created by Jae Kwon, Zarko Milosevic, and Ethan Buchman.

While it's not necessary to understand every technical detail be-hind these blockchain networks, it's worth understanding that interoperability will play a big part in how DeFi develops in the future.

We are already starting to see how DeFi projects are allowing their users to swap between blockchains without the need to under-stand the specifics of how this action occurs. This trend will con-tinue and accelerate over time, as interoperability becomes more and more established and cross-chain movements are abstracted away from the user experience.

Interoperability will allow users to hold collateral-type assets se-curely on one chain while taking advantage of the transaction or user experience benefits of another chain, without needing to be technical at all. The Compound CASH system in development at the moment is a good example of early innovation in this space and something that we are likely to see a lot more of in the future.

Layer 2 Scalability

The question of scaling the Ethereum network to allow it to han-dle more transactions without gas fees spiking is not a new one. However, just as the DeFi bull run has increased the focus on cross chain solutions and interoperability, it has also meant that layer 2 solutions are increasingly being discussed.

Layer 2 solutions are chain-specific scaling solutions that use a sidechain of the main chain. Transactions can be calculated and batched on a sidechain before being completed in one go on the main chain, thereby reducing the cost of multiple transactions into only one.

A good way of thinking about this process is to compare it to how an accountant might create a ledger on a spreadsheet. While the main functions and formulas are incorporated into the spread-sheet, the accountant will probably also use a pen to make small additions and subtractions on a piece of paper, which can then be added to the main spreadsheet in order to produce a finalized ledger. In this analogy, the spreadsheet is the main chain and the paper is the layer 2 sidechain.

L2 Scalability Adoption

Project	Technology	Ecosystem Products		
zkSync	zkRollup	LOOPRING	AAVE	Balancer
		1inch	coinbase	Huobi
		BINANCE	MoonPay	ripio
		argent	imToken	MYKEY
		flexa	CoinGecko	STORJ
		StablePay	golem	GITCOIN
		numio	Curve	
LOOPRING	zkRollup	GITCOIN	RAILS	pNetwork
STARKWARE	zk-STARK	DeversiFi	iMMUTABLE	dYdX
Aztec	zk-SNARK	Zcash	DUSK	MatterLabs
Optimism	Optimistic Rollup	SYNTHETIX EXCHANGE	coinbase	Uniswap
Hermez	zkRollup	———		

Well-known layer 2 solutions include zkSync (created by Matter Labs), Starkware and Optimism. Vitalik Buterin, the creator of Ethereum, has personally given his support to both zkSync and Optimism, but all these solutions can be used to increase scalability. For example, traders might put limit orders on a sidechain, which can be made if someone else can be matched against the trade or released if no takers appear.

Increasing DeFi Projects' Flexibility and Functional Updates of DeFi projects

As DeFi is a highly competitive and innovative environment, projects have to constantly update their functionality to satisfy as many user requirements as possible. Even if a project is well known in the community and had a large industry influence in the past, that doesn't mean users will be loyal forever.

Uniswap is a great example of how a large, successful DeFi project follows market trends and pushes innovations to improve user experience and facilitate the overall DeFi adoption.

Uniswap V3

In order to keep its leading market positions, the project introduces Version 3. The two main advantages of the new version are concentrated liquidity and multiple fee tiers.

Concentrated liquidity is going to allow liquidity providers to control the price ranges within which their funds can be allocated. This control creates a set of individual positions combined in a single pool where users can trade.

Multiple fee tiers are introduced to compensate risks LPs take in accordance with the degree of those risks.

The updates enable:

- Liquidity provision with up to 4000x investment efficiency compared to V2

- Low-slippage trade execution
- Lowering the downside risk of preferred assets
- Improvement of the time-weighted average price (TWAP) oracles, where any TWAP within the past ~9 days can be calculated in a single on-chain call
- Decreasing gas costs through deployment of the L 2 Optimism solution

With the introduction of these new features, the Uniswap team is striving to offer users the most flexible and advantageous AMM.

Project Partnerships

Increasingly, projects are partnering with one another where they see synergies between their stated aims and the users they serve.

A DeFi partnership or merger is very different from one that occurs in traditional finance. In traditional finance, such events usually require one dominant party to acquire the assets and rights of the other entity, or they require the foundation of a newly-integrated entity, where stakeholders share rights and control. DeFi partnerships and mergers are usually based on a highly flexible set of terms for both parties.

Usually, a partnership in DeFi will seem advantageous if it can generate the following benefits:

- Greater economies of scale
- Acquisition of developer talent
- Increased promotion of the projects involved

Not all partnerships and mergers are the same, though, so it's worth looking at a few early examples of how some of them have occurred in practice.

The Yearn Finance Ecosystem

Yearn Finance is an outstanding example of this trend in DeFi, as the project has performed a range of strategic partnerships and structural transformations. It's aim has been to become a multi-purpose DeFi platform that offers a wide range of services. This diversification has already drawn the attention of Yield Farmers.

It could be said that Yearn Finance started the trend for partnerships as far back as its launch. The cooperation it enabled with Curve Finance on the development of its yPool and YFI Balancer pool resulted in a massive increase in awareness among the DeFi community and was covered at length by crypto media outlets and within forum discussions. Presumably, the success of this partnership led Yearn Finance to investigate how similar moves could positively affect the project too.

More recently, Yearn Finance extended its ecosystem with four other DeFi projects in the space of one week, merging with Pickle Finance, CREAM, and Cover, and partnering with PowerPool.

Through the merger with CREAM, Yearn Finance wanted to develop and implement a more complex network of lending protocols to function as a highly effective lending market. The Yearn Finance team will be involved in the development of CREAM V2, which is aimed at designing products for lending and leverage. Moreover, the flagship Yield Farming/Pickle Finance product, the pickle jars, will be integrated into the V2-vaults.

Yearn Finance has also stepped into the field of smart contract coverage through its merger with Cover Protocol. This project focuses on hedging against the risks inherent to Farming and staking, and Yearn Finance founder Andre Cronje was already advising the project before the merger was agreed. Probably the most significant merger for the Yield Farming community, though, was the one Yearn Finance initiated with SushiSwap just after these announcements. This strategy was focused on putting together the best technical features of both platforms in order to offer a better infrastructure, combining total value locked into a single pool of assets and benefiting from common developer resources. Yearn is clearly considering both horizontal and vertical approaches in its merger strategies.

Horizontal mergers are aimed at increasing market share and consolidating development resources. Vertical mergers are focused on incorporating different companies into single vertically integrated structures. Within these new structures, different entities can continue developing their regular products and services, but they also become integrated into one combined supply chain. The goal is to achieve synergies, and the Sushiswap, Cover, and Cream mergers all fall into this latter category of vertical mergers.

DEXes Extend Their Trading Tools

Interest in decentralized exchanges has gradually increased over time among traders for a number of reasons. One of the most important factors is that they fit more comfortably into the idea of decentralized finance than their centralized counterparts because you don't have to give up custody of your assets to a centralized third party, which could lose them in an attack or seize them from you.

Although the number of DEX users has exploded, a few UI-related obstacles remain that DEXes have to overcome to keep attracting new users. Various DeFi projects are innovating in this direction, and user experience improvements are being made on an ongoing basis.

For example, most DEXes have added limit orders and decentralized order books recently, with one example being dYdX. These changes allow users to buy or sell assets at a specific price and remove the need to rely on market orders, which expose them to greater trading risks during volatile periods. If volatility is high or if a trade takes a long time to execute, users can experience large price slippages that affect their investment strategies. Limit orders negate this issue, and when implemented on DEXes they are totally non-custodial, which ensures users stay in control of their assets throughout.

Trading volume on Ethereum-based DEXes

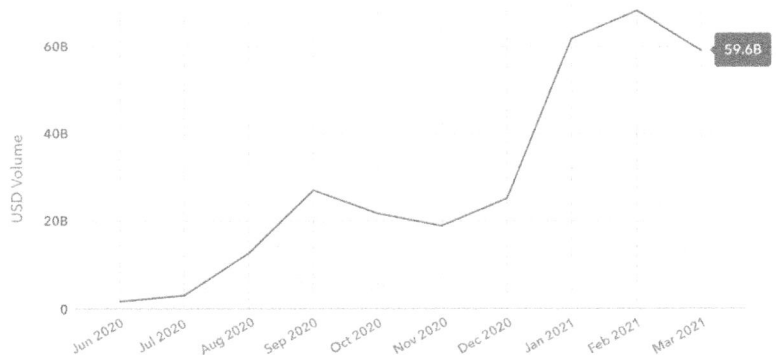

Another feature that DEXes are adding is stop orders. This feature allows users to perform a desired transaction without having to reach a certain price level. Instead, they specify an exact price at which their buy or sell order will be automatically executed, and they are thereby able to manage risk.

Finally, a lot of DEXes are also working on enabling margin trading. Essentially, this element allows traders to leverage funds in order to multiply their purchasing power. As with the other features mentioned, margin trading on DEXes is much more advantageous than on centralized exchanges because users don't need to trust a third party and share personal information and also because no hidden fees are present.

DeFiYield is also at the forefront of innovation in this space, with a host of new, relevant tools. These tools include the L2 Dex Aggregator, which allows for cross-chain crypto sw'aps at the best rates, and Cross-chain Spot Trading, which includes real-time trading charts, limit orders, asset leveraging, fast withdrawals, and a potential for short positions

Adoption of Seigniorage Coins

While the hype around these digital assets was temporary, the journey they are on is far from over, as they represent a new way of optimizing monetary policies for cryptocurrencies.

If you're still uncertain about what differentiates these assets, one key feature to understand about them is that they are algorithmic stablecoins, which means their value is not collateralized with any asset and is instead adjusted algorithmically through certain supply dynamics. One of the main reasons they are so important is because they may provide a solution to the problems of using cryptocurrencies as a store of value and medium of exchange.

Seigniorage coins define the optimal coin supply through the separation of the demand for a coin into speculative demand and transactional demand.

The benefits that seigniorage coins might provide to the DeFi ecosystem in future are as follows:

- Autonomy from outside markets

- Decentralization

- Stable value that protects against volatility

- No reliance on tangible assets

- Ability to integrate with any DeFi application

New seigniorage coin projects continue to emerge, which is leading to a distinct new DeFi sector that is worth keeping an eye on, even though the initial hype has passed.

NFTs

Non-fungible tokens (NFTs) are totally unique assets that cannot be duplicated or divided.

They differ from other tokens, such as Bitcoin, which are fungible because each individual token is exactly the same. Just like one dollar can be swapped for one dollar, one bitcoin can be swapped for one bitcoin and this like-for-like exchangeability is key to a token being fungible.

NFTs have been around for some time and are the technology behind CryptoKitties, which received a lot of coverage in the 2017 bull run. They have developed a lot since then, though, and the strong belief behind the hype is that because NFTs create digital scarcity, they can be used to revolutionize how music, art, content, collectibles and many other unique goods are owned and purchased.

The majority of current activity is occurring across the most well-known NFT marketplaces, which are Rarible, OpenSea, Mintbase, and Nifty Gateway.

The 2021 NFT Hype

NFTs caught the public's attention in a big way in 2021, mainly because of the celebrities, influencers, and artists who have been promoting them. Such examples demonstrate that this trend for the future is already happening now.

Record NFT Digital Art Sales

Even now, digital art is being sold at extraordinary prices. Beeple set a record price for a piece of NFT digital art, when his "EVERY-DAYS: THE FIRST 5000 DAYS" sold for the equivalent of $69.3m (40,652 ETH) through renowned auction house Christie's.

Crypto art volumes by marketplace in USD

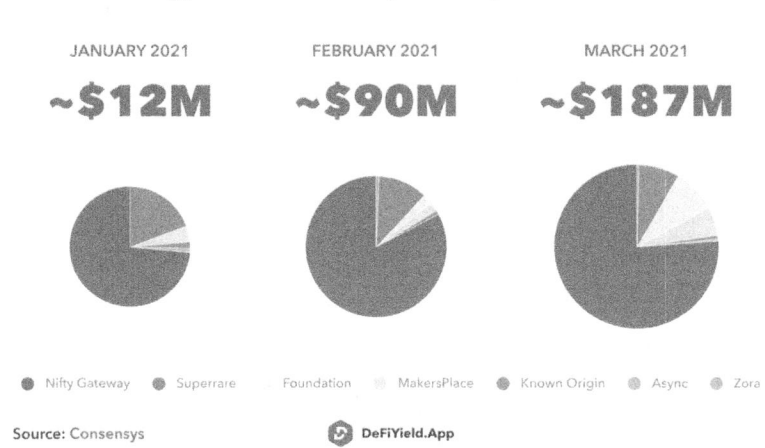

JANUARY 2021	FEBRUARY 2021	MARCH 2021
~$12M	~$90M	~$187M

● Nifty Gateway ● Superrare Foundation MakersPlace ● Known Origin ● Async ● Zora

Source: Consensys   DeFiYield.App

This deal followed his sale of other artwork for large amounts, including CROSSROADS, which sold for $6.6m (3,869 ETH), and THE COMPLETE MF COLLECTION, which sold for $777,777 (456 ETH). Other artists who have managed to sell NFT digital art for significant amounts include Pak, Steveaoki and Antonitudisco.

Celebrity Endorsements

Many of the richest people in the world who have already declared an interest in bitcoin, cryptocurrencies, and DeFi, are also showing the same interest in NFTs.

These people include Jack Dorsey, who sold his first tweet as an NFT for over $2.9 million, Elon Musk, who planned to sell a techno song as an NFT before withdrawing, and Mark Cuban, who has declared that he has invested in NFT platform Mintable. Grimes, an artist and Elon Musk's partner, has sold off various images and videos for the equivalent of $6 million.

Other social media influencers involved in NFTs include Logan Paul, who has sold over $5 million NFTs, and Gary Vee, an investor and entrepreneur who has said he believes NFTs will be the gateway into crypto for the masses.

In addition to artists and celebrities selling rare pieces of art and music as NFTs, some well-known brands are using their exclusive content licences to generate NFT digital collectibles.

Probably the best known of these brands is NBA Topshots, which are the officially licensed digital collectibles of the US National Basketball Association. The items being sold are short videos of significant shots or plays within games, which are "marked at creation with a unique serial number, with guaranteed scarcity and protected ownership guaranteed by the blockchain."

The most expensive topshots, which include players such as LeBron James, Ja Morant, and Zion Williamson, are trading for over $200,000 on the platform's marketplace.

The Future of NFTs

While both the total potential value of the NFT market and the specific value of individual items is very difficult to assess right now, this is definitely a part of the crypto markets that you should keep an eye on. It's also worth understanding a couple of dynamics that may result in the NFT industry operating in a slightly different way to many other areas of DeFi.

First, the unique nature of an NFT means it is very unlikely that a regulatory body would see it as a security. NFTs are more likely to be treated as a commodity, which means less potential difficulties for the issuer and therefore more likelihood that a greater number of issuers, including celebrities, artists, and influencers, will be attracted to this space.

Second, you should also consider that the NFT prices will likely be uncorrelated to other crypto markets. Correlation has been a big part of crypto markets as they have grown over the last decade, but NFTs are likely to be uncorrelated to other cryptocurrency and token prices, just as fine art is uncorrelated to gold or stocks.

Security Concerns

For all of the positive trends that are emerging within Yield Farming, please note that security concerns do persist.

As the market innovates, some of this innovation will bring about more technologically complex projects that require more sophisticated investment strategies. Yield Farmers should be aware of this complexity and make sure they research all opportunities thoroughly if they are to avoid opening themselves up to new security risks. Furthermore, they should be aware that as DeFi grows, smart contract auditing cannot slip. The industry is currently lacking in qualified smart contract developers and auditors,which is a real risk of which users should be aware.

Another issue to be aware of as DeFi and the wider crypto markets grow is the threat that cyber attackers pose. Users need to stay alert to spot any scam projects these attackers might develop in order to steal funds. They should also take care to always keep their identities hidden.

Of course, all of these precautions should not stop you from taking advantage of the benefits that Yield Farming provides. It's a matter of "forewarned is forearmed." The best way to remain up to date with any security issues you should avoid is through DeFi-Yield.App, which has all the tools and resources you need to safely succeed at Yield Farming..

MAIN TAKEAWAYS FROM THIS CHAPTER

DeFi is a highly innovative environment that attracts users and investors from all over the world due to the wide range of advantages it has over traditional finance.

Because DeFi projects are constantly introducing new solutions to improve user experience, offer higher returns to investors and mitigate security concerns, the industry is expected to keep its impressive growth pace in the long term.

The most significant trends in DeFi development include decentralized governance enhancements, an increase in cross-chain solutions, partnerships between projects and increasing adoption of Binance Smart Chain and Huobi ECO Chain.

Other important trends include Layer 2 solutions that can reduce gas prices on Ethereum, increasing the flexibility and competitiveness of DeFi projects, DEXes evolving to compete with centralized exchanges and the growth of NFTs.

Finally, it's worth noting some of the key trends that DEFIYIELD is leading, which include fighting security concerns through community synergy, informing users about potential financial threats, auditing DeFi projects and introducing automated tools to check smart contract security.

VIII. WHY YOU SHOULD USE DEFIYIELD NOW

At the very start of this book, I included a quote from Mark Cuban, the billionaire internet entrepreneur. He said that DeFi is straightforward if you understand the principles and try it for yourself. In the same interview, he also gave the following message to the DeFi industry:

"If you don't take care of the little guy, it's going to backfire on the whole [DeFi] industry."

Taking care of all of our users as they journey through the exciting world of DeFi is exactly what we are all about at DeFiYield.

Throughout *The Wall Street Era is Over,* we have outlined in detail the principles for safely succeeding at Yield Farming. By reading this book, you have already significantly reduced your risk exposure.

The Problems DeFiYield Solves for DeFi Users

Many issues still remain for Yield Farmers, which can be summarized as follows:

- Accessibility - Many projects' poor user experience, coupled with the need to use and understand many different and unfamiliar tools, makes DeFi difficult to access.

- Complexity - You need to have a lot of foundational knowledge, and you must keep up with a large amount of new information if you are going to succeed.

- Security - Defects in smart contracts and scammer presence mean that users must constantly be aware of DeFi's risks.

Solving these problems for users is the heart of what we do. DeFiYield is a unique platform with many features designed to help you access, manage, and secure your DeFi assets through a single, user-friendly portal. We are constantly updating and improving the solutions at DeFiYield, and new tools are always in development.

Please visit us at https://DeFiYield.App/ to see the latest ways in which we're improving DeFi. If you have found The Wall Street Era is Over useful, we expect you'll feel the same way about DeFiYield!

IX. CONCLUSION

——

Time for Next Steps

You've reached the end of *The Wall Street Era is Over*, but this is just the beginning of your journey.

Hopefully, you're excited about what's coming next for you in DeFi, and maybe you've already joined the party. Since you've read this far, we assume you see the enormous potential of an informed approach to DeFi, which stands to make a positive impact on the finances of everyone who participates.

In turn, it's easy to see why DeFi is poised to create change for the better throughout the world economy. This is Finance 3.0 at its most advanced, an astonishing convergence of money and computer code, contracts that can execute on their own, and trustless environments where no central authority is needed. That combination means banking without middlemen and finance without friction. It truly is a revolution.

Throughout *The Wall Street Era is Over*, our goal has been to empower you to take part. We've told you our own story — the good, the bad, and the ugly — and why DeFi is so important to us. You should have a firm grasp now of what makes DeFi different from anything else, the protocols that form its foundation, and the projects that are propelling it. We've dealt with decentralized governance and even lived through vampire attacks!

From there, we've tried to show you where you fit in. Are you a cautious investor, or are you risk-on or degen? What do you need to know in order to properly size up a DeFi investment opportunity? From those generalities, we zero in on the specifics, so you can apply these universal principles before you invest in particular projects.

That's when we draw back the curtain on the heart of DeFi for the individual investor: Yield Farming. Yield Farming is what we're most excited about – it's where the opportunity in DeFi truly lies, and also the danger.

As you can see, we have not tried to give you a one-dimensional view of Yield Farming. Naturally, we are DeFi enthusiasts, but that doesn't mean we think it's for everybody. On the one hand, Yield Farming has the appeal of high returns, composable "money Legos" that form fascinating new financial structures, and much more growth to come. On the other hand, Yield Farming can be hard. Many of the tools are still in their infancy and are difficult to use. The process comes with the risk of extreme volatility, scams, and (for now) scant consequences for the scammers.

It's Your Turn

Once you made it that far, we shared what has made us successful – our strategies. Our hope is that The Wall Street Era is Over as a playbook will not only enrich you financially, but also make you want to be a part of the larger DeFi community. At its best, the Yield Farming community are people who want to help each other learn and succeed.

Even the best investors, from traditional finance to DeFi, lose money some days. We certainly have! It's OK if those losses come as a result of the inevitable ups and downs of value changing hands via a level playing field.

Where it is definitely NOT OK, however, is if your losses come at the hands of scammers whose line of business is to trick you and steal your money. We've done everything we can to alert you to this possibility. As painful as it was, we've told you our own story of getting scammed so you'll understand our motivations. It was bad enough that it happened to us – we don't want it to happen to you.

This book outlines steps for you to stay safe, and DeFiYield's tools go even further. Please use them! Your safety in the DeFi space is paramount because without security this vital financial sector cannot grow.

Things change fast in crypto, and NFTs are a great example of that. Although NFTs are not part of DeFi, strictly speaking, we included them because they're a perfect demonstration of how a crypto sector can suddenly explode in both attention and value, as they did in Q1 2021.

Something that seemed like a fun diversion, as NFTs first did when they debuted as CryptoKitties in 2017, can suddenly become very serious business. That potential holds true throughout crypto, including in DeFi. Our point is, if something catches your eye, keep track of it – you never know when it might catch on.

The last section is all about DeFiYield's tools. We didn't want this book to be a veiled sales pitch for DeFiYield – it's first and foremost a guide for Yield Farmers to go deeper into the space and do so safely. We've told you about a wide range of tools, and we've even included "competing" platforms in these pages. You should choose the ones that feel best to you.

But when you try out what we've built at DeFiYield – such as the

Cross-Chain Asset Management Dashboard, Yield Farming Optimizer, and especially DeFiYield Safe – we hope you'll feel the spiritual connection between our platform and this book. We created them to make DeFi a better place – not just profitable, but safe, stimulating, and exhilarating to explore. All we need now is YOU.

X. GLOSSARY OF TERMS

APR - Stands for Annual Percentage Rate. It is the interest rate that is charged on a financial product over a year. Commonly used in traditional finance to show how much a consumer will pay over a year for a loan, mortgage or outstanding credit card amount.

APY - Stands for Annual Percentage Yield. It is the interest rate someone receives from an investment product over a year. Commonly used in decentralized finance to show how much a yield farmer can receive over a year when using their digital assets to provide liquidity.

Arbitrage - Benefiting from price differences of an asset between two markets. The profit is made from purchasing the asset on the exchange with the lower price and selling it for a higher price on the second exchange.

Backdoor - A deliberate security weakening of a smart contract aimed at deceiving manipulations with user funds. This term refers to situations when devs introduce functions and conditions of their execution to the code that allow them to control user assets, including transferring them to any wanted addresses seamlessly and at any time.

Bear market - a period of time when participants in a financial market are generally considered to have a negative outlook about the price of assets over the foreseeable future. The opposite of a bull run.

Bull run - a period of time when participants in a financial market are generally considered to have a positive outlook about the price of assets over the foreseeable future. The opposite of a bear market.

Collateralization - Backing the value of one asset with the use of another asset. In the context of DeFi, this process is associated with locking collateralized assets on a blockchain protocol. Usually, collateralization is used to secure loans or maintain the value of stablecoins.

Crypto wallet - A software or a device that stores public and private keys and allows users to store, send, receive, and monitor various blockchain tokens.

Custodial and non-custodial - Classifications of financial services provided to users for storage and management of their assets, where presence of the third party control over these assets is the main criterion for referring a service to one of the classes. In DeFi, non-custodial means that users can control their own crypto without being dependent on any external entity that would be responsible for management of the assets held and thereby constantly expose users to the risk of security issues, conflict of interests, or betrayal.

DAO (decentralized autonomous organization) - A way of structuring an organization to run based on rules encoded on a blockchain. All decisions are made through voting of network participants. Transactions are executed automatically and only if all predefined required terms are met. No centralized guidance or control takes place in such a system.

Etherscan - A block explorer that allows analyzing transactions to be performed on Ethereum.

Ethereum network transaction fees - Since every transaction on Ethereum requires computational resources to execute, each transaction requires a fee. Ethereum network transaction fees are paid in gas to the miners who verify and process transactions.

Epoch - A division of time used in a blockchain protocol.

DEX (Decentralized Exchange) - A digital platform designed to allow its users to buy and sell cryptocurrency assets peer-to-peer, based on a set of conditions encoded on a blockchain. All offered services are provided automatically, without participation of centralized intermediaries. Usually, DEXes are run by decentralized governance.

FOMO (Fear of missing out) - A form of anxiety experienced by cryptocurrency market participants that comes from a belief that peers might be benefiting from a possibly favorable event or a hyped project. People experiencing FOMO feel an urgent need to mimic what everybody around them is doing.

Gas - The fee that is required to conduct a transaction or a smart contract on a blockchain.

Gwei - The smallest unit of Ether (ETH) - the Ethereum network's cryptocurrency. One gwei is equal to 0.000000001 ETH.

ICO (Initial Coin Offering) - A capital-raising process initiated by a crypto project.

KYC - Stands for Know-Your-Customer. These are checks that mostly take place in traditional finance because financial regulators have mandated that financial institutions must check the identity of their users before they can facilitate payments for them.

Ledger - A system that stores data about financial transactions.

Blockchains function like distributed ledgers: they consist of a variety of nodes that process and verify every transaction, generating records and creating a veracity consensus.

Leverage - A trading or investment tool that refers to borrowing funds in order to increase purchasing power and generate higher returns.

Liquidation - Distributing a borrower's assets to a claimant when the required collateralization ratio is not maintained.

Liquidity pool - A pool of tokens locked in a smart contract and used as a source of liquidity for trading operations, lending, borrowing, and other services offered by decentralized Apps.

Liquidity - The ease with which an asset can be converted to cash without having significant influence on its price in the selected market. In the crypto industry, liquidity usually refers to the trading volume in a market.

Margin trading - Borrowing funds from a third party with the purpose of increasing the purchasing power of trading operations.

Metamask - A popular cryptocurrency wallet that allows users to interact with distributed applications based on the Ethereum blockchain.

Oracles - Third-party services that blockchain protocols use as sources of external real-world data.

Order book - A list of buy and sell orders (bids and asks) for a specific asset placed by market participants at specific prices. Information about prices from order books is critical for investment and trading decisions.

Pre-mining - A process that involves issuing a cryptocurrency asset before a project is launched and its blockchain protocol is deployed. As project owners or core developers control pre-mining, it can be considered a controversial step on the project's roadmap. Pre-mined funds can not only be used as a reserve pool, ensuring financial soundness of the project, but they can also be distributed among a small number of people who will have significant influence on the project's development and on its tokens' market price, if the receivers of the pre-mined funds decide to sell them on the open market.

Proof of concept - An early and often lightweight manifestation of a strategy, such as an app,website or service, that has been developed to prove the validity of a theory or idea.

Proof of stake (PoS) - A mechanism used to reach consensus about the data stored on a blockchain. The validators involved in confirming the state of the blockchain are chosen based on the amount of tokens they stake. Proof of Stake differs from Proof of Work, which involves miners solving complicated mathematical problems in order to be chosen as the validator who confirms the blockchain state.

Private key - An algorithmic password, automatically generated by a blockchain wallet, that is required to access cryptocurrency assets and conduct transactions with them.

Rekt - A DeFi slang word derived from "wrecked" that describes a tremendous fund loss resulting from investment or trade. It may also refer to situations when the value of a crypto asset collapses.

Rug pull - An unexpected theft of token liquidity provided by project investors that is performed by scammers through malicious strategy contracts.

Scalability - The property of a blockchain to handle an increasing number of transactions without decreasing the processing speed. The higher scalability of a network, the better it can react to the rising demand.

Slippage - The difference between the expected price of a trade execution and the actual price of the trade execution, which can occur as a result of the delay between the time points of the placing and its completion. This effect can be expected when a user places market orders during high market volatility or when the order size doesn't correspond to the demand for the traded asset.

Smart contract - A transaction agreements' set of encoded terms that executes automatically through validation on a selected blockchain when the terms are met. Information about executed transactions is stored on the blockchain, and users can track it.

Smart contract ownership - this refers to the network address (for example, an Ethereum address) that was used to deploy the smart contract and any other addresses that were set as the owner of the smart contract afterwards. Smart contract owners may have special privileges to call certain functions, depending on how the smart contract was written.

Stablecoin - A cryptocurrency that's value is linked to an outside, more stable asset, such as fiat, for stabilization of its price, which allows participants of the cryptocurrency market to use it as a store-of-value. Stablecoins can be backed with fiat, commodity, cryptocurrency, or they can be algo-based, meaning their value is maintained automatically by an algorithm encoded on a blockchain protocol.

Store-of-Value - An asset that's value remains unaltered over time without depreciating. Therefore, it can be used as a reliable means of saving purchasing power for future transactions.

Token - A crypto asset designed with a specific utility for accessing and using certain blockchain.

Volatility - A degree of the price change of an asset within an analyzed timeframe, which creates profit opportunities or can cause losses. The larger the price swing, the higher volatility.

Web 3.0 - The next step of the internet. Web 1.0 was the early, static web, and Web 2.0 was the social but centralized web that big tech dominates. Web 3.0 is decentralized and powered by crypto.

Whale - An individual or an entity that possesses large enough funds to move prices for crypto assets, traded on a specific market. Whales can use their huge financial potential to make profits by manipulating prices.

Whitepaper - A technical document issued by a blockchain project that explains its purpose and uniqueness, outlines its main features, and presents the applied technology. This document may be updated at certain development stages of the project.

WHO ARE WE?

DeFiYield is the world's only Safe Defi Cross-Chain Asset Management Protocol Based on Machine Learning that aims at securing the rapidly growing Decentralized Finance industry from serious threats. We have designed the safest and most accessible DeFi yield farming ecosystem available today.

Our experts are also the leading independent auditors of smart contracts in the DeFi industry. With 40 audits completed, all of which cover projects requested by the DeFi community rather than paid for by development teams.

Such a complex product is developed by a multinational team, consisting of 50+ specialists and growing, that have diverse expertise in distributed ledger technologies, payment solutions, security domain, computer science, and other fields.

Made in the USA
Monee, IL
11 February 2022